Fantastic Alfa Romeo

Fantastic Alfa Romeo

Photography by Sandro Bacchi
Translated from the Italian by Eric Dregni

Motorbooks International
Publishers & Wholesalers ®

This edition published 1996 by Motorbooks International Publishers and Wholesalers, 729 Prospect Avenue, PO Box 1, Osceola, WI 54020 USA

Previously published in 1992 by Giorgio Nada Editore, Vimodrone (Milan)

© 1992 Giorgio Nada Editore
© Motorbooks International Engish Edition

Library of Congress Cataloging-in-Publication Data Available.

ISBN 0-7603-0237-5

On the front cover: This 1960 750 Series Giulietta Sprint Veloce is a transition car, featuring an early transmission and engine. Photographer David Gooley is the second owner. *David Gooley*

On the back cover: A rare and prized black 1940 6C 2500 Super Sport Berlina—not your everyday Alfa Romeo.

A 1958 750 Series Giulietta Spider Veloce, featuring Pinin Farina coachwork and Weber carburetors.

Shown in race trim is this 1967 Giulia GTA Junior, a competition car slotted between the GT Junior and the GTA. It features a 1600cc engine based on that of the GTA.

Grille and badge from a 1993 164. The 164s debuted in 1987, representing Alfa Romeo's first front-wheel-drive flagship car. *David Gooley*

Printed in Hong Kong

Editorial coordination
Daniele Antonietti

Editing
Laura Negri

Graphics
Studio Tre s.r.l.

Photography
Sandro Bacchi (color)

Giorgio Nada Editore Archives

Centro Documentazione Alfa Romeo, Arese

Dedication
This book grew out of an idea of the Italian Alfa Romeo Registry (RIAR), in particular its president, Stefano d'Amico, from whom appeared in 1988 a similar volume dedicated to 33 legendary Ferraris. Within its 80 year history, the House of Biscione has created more than 33 cars that could considered legendary, but this number resonates so magically that the editor couldn't resist it.

The RIAR created a commission to select which of the vast number of deserving cars would be included in the book. There are some models, certainly, that might have been included, but for a variety of reasons we did not have the good fortune to have an example in good enough condition to warrant inclusion in this volume. It was never anyone's intention to discriminate in any way against any model not included here.

The duty of guiding the commission fell to Gigi Bonfanti, whose enthusiasm and dedication to the marque of Biscione made the resulting book possible. To him, therefore, this book is dedicated.

Acknowledgments
The author and editor wish to thank Stefano d'Amico, president of the Italian Alfa Romeo Registry, who promoted this book, and Maurizio Tabucchi, president of the technical commission A.S.I. and RIAR. Particular thanks go to Alfa Romeo, in the persons of Roberto Benvenuti, Marino Bussi, Antonio Magro and Vittorio Meloni, for their willing availability and constant support, and with them, thanks to the Centro Documentazione Alfa Romeo and the Alfa Romeo History Museum of Arese. And finally, we must mention the owners of the cars featured in this volume, whose tremendous courtesy and patience made the photography go smoothly and successfully. For all those who are not singled out by name, we offer hearty thanks to everyone.

CONTENTS

INTRODUCTION

——

The unfortunate and short-lived adventure of Alexander Darracq and his Italian cars would have been an insignificant footnote to the history of automobiles if the founder of the make hadn't interfered and moved the factory from Naples to Milan in 1907. He owned a large expanse of land in the countryside of Lombardy just outside Milan, upon which he established his factory. The factory was named "Portello" after the huge double doors of the nearby Sforza castle, built in the year 500 AD. The location was in a big field just past the road "Via Mario Pagano" and next to the ancient road "Portello," also named for the famous doors.

These were difficult times in which to lay the foundation for an automobile factory. In the United States, the car had already been put in center stage as the transportation of the future. In Italy, however, automobiles were seen as a luxury of the rich and Italians were suspicious of this new means of transportation, Therefore, the Società Italiana Automobili Darracq fell on hard times beginning in the Fall of 1907, and within two years, a management crisis nearly caused it to go under.

This was the perfect opportunity for rich investors from Lombardy to salvage the company, rehabilitate the factory, and produce a much more ambitious concept in cars. Ugo Stella, the new managing director of the company, chose Giuseppe Merosi of La Bianchi to design two new highly advanced cars. On June 24, 1910, the revamped company was named Anonima Lombarda Fabbrica Automobili, or ALFA for short. Merosi's design of the first car, named the 24 hp, was completed within just a few months and featured the new ALFA coat of arms on the radiator. The new emblem combined two coats of arms: the red cross on white field of the city of Milan and the coiled serpent of the Lombard viscounts who had invested in the company.

In spite of the promising debut of the 24 hp and the less powerful 12 hp, times had already taken a turn for the worse. The economic boom had already soured by 1914, and by the Summer of 1915, exports were blocked due to the outbreak of hostilities in Europe. The situation looked bleak for ALFA with the rough economic conditions of World War I.

Luckily, an extremely successful Neapolitan engineer named Nicola Romeo took over the factory and converted it to the production of war materiel. He had previously made a living importing and building highly technical machinery, so he was ideally suited to help ALFA survive the war years. In December of 1915, ALFA changed hands, but it wasn't until February of 1918 that it officially became "Alfa Romeo." Finally, in 1920, the new name appeared all over the car: on the hood, the engine, etc. After all the transitions of World War I, the factory could once again turn its attention to what it knew best: the manufacture of automobiles.

A new day had dawned for Alfa and the factory at Portello. On the racetrack, the red Alfas decorated with their quadrifoglio emblems became the cars to be reckoned with. From the 1920s until the difficult years of World War II, the racetrack was dominated by Alfa Romeo.

From the exceptional RL SS to the surprising P2, from the monumental dynasty of the 6C 1750 and the 8C 2300 until the triumph of the P3 and the 158/159, there was always an Alfa Romeo to compete with on the racetrack.

Winning races became the raison d'être for Alfa Romeo. Some of Alfa's many successes from this period included 5 World Championships, 11 Mille Miglias, 10 Targa Florios, 9 European Touring Championships, 5 Formula Three European Championships, and numerous national titles. Alfa Romeo has won more competitions than any other kind of automobile; the long history of Alfa Romeo, therefore, is synonymous with the long history of the automobile.

An extremely high level of planning on all models at the Portello factory produced such unforgettable cars as the 2500, the postwar 1900, the fantastic Giuliettas and Giulias, and the other models that preceded today's Alfas.

The long list of famous cars won numerous international races and made Alfa extremely popular with millions of fans. Pictured in this book, is a select group of models that have survived due to the loving care of a few private collectors and the wonderful Alfa Romeo Museum of Arese. We didn't choose the cars because they are the most famous, the most elegant, or the ones that won the most races. Rather, the cars in these pages were chosen because they contributed to the entire story of the marque. These are the cars that, in 50 years, have turned the pages of automotive history for many reasons to construct a legend. Or, to be precise, the legendary Alfa Romeo.

Luciano Greggio

24 HP: A DASHING DEBUT

The 24 HP, used as transport for military commanders during World War I, is shown here during the advance of Montello.

The first car produced by ALFA was the 24 HP designed by Giuseppe Merosi in 1910. While the mechanicals of the car may not have been revolutionary,

the styling was. The four cylinder 4084 cc (100x130 mm) monobloc engine had a compression of 4.15:1 and delivered 42 hp at 2200 rpm. The weight of the motor was reduced by fitting a smaller flywheel and by drilling the piston skirts. The mixture was fed through a Zenith updraft carburetor and was ignited via a high tension magneto rather than a battery.

The transmission of the 24 HP consisted of a four-speed gearbox coupled to a torque tube drive to the solid rear axle, all of which was extremely advanced for the time. The chassis, on the other hand, was much more conventional with the side rails and cross braces of stamped steel. Both front and rear rigid axles rode on semi-elliptic springs. The brakes were mechanical with the transmission brake operated by the foot pedal and the rear brakes operated by the hand lever, all of which was typical of the era.

The 24 HP had its debut in the Autumn of 1910 and was soon well known due to its quick acceleration and outstanding handling. The powerful and robust engine pushed the car to 100 kmph making it one of the famed grand touring cars of its day. Compared to other ALFAs, the 24 HP had

one of the longest production runs at Portello. Between 1910 and 1920, 680 of them were produced in five different series. The first two series were the A and the B of which 50 were built between 1910 and 1911. In the next two years, 200 of the C and D series were produced with a slight increase in engine power from 42 hp to 45 hp. In 1914, the horsepower was upped again to 49 hp on the E series and the cam shaft drive was changed from gears to silent chain operation. Because of these changes, the 380 examples of the E series became known as the 20/30 hp model.

As was to be expected, it was the wealthy who especially took to the 24 HP. But, because of its practicality, the model was also used by military commanders.

Since the 24 HP was so widely accepted for its performance and durability, ALFA saw the potential to turn it into a racer. Just one year after the introduction of the 24 HP, ALFA was busy preparing a pair of its cars for the sixth Targa Florio. This competition took place on the "Grande Circuito delle Madonie" in the mountains of Sicily on May 14, 1911.

The spider da corsa version of the 24 HP featured 3 hp more and weighed 130 kg less than the touring version of the car, while its top speed was increased to 110 kmph. In its first race, Giuseppe Campari was headed for certain victory when his goggles became obscured by a spray of mud two laps from the finish.

When World War I hit Italy in 1915, ALFA's mechanics were forced to turn their attention to building functional war vehicles. All was not wasted, however, since after the war the 20/30 HP cars developed into the 20/30 HP ES Sport model. Between 1921 and 1922, 124 of these cars were built. Their 4250 cc engines provided 67 hp. The 20/30 HP is considered to be a direct descendant of the 24 HP.

The 20/30 HP pictured on these pages is at the Alfa Romeo Museo Storico in Arese and is one of the very few that have survived from the first series of 1910. The elegant bodywork is signed by Castagna, a well-known designer and builder of horse carriages. The tradition of the marque of the serpent was augmented by the team of Alfa Romeo and Castagna through hard work and the complementing of each other's style and designs.

RL: THE WORK OF A CHAMPION

Top:
An archive photo of the
RL chassis.
Above:
The RL with Prince
Umberto in 1927.

The RL model was conceived and designed by Giuseppe Merosi in 1920. With a wheelbase of 344 cm and a track of 144 cm, the chassis was conventional with a frame of pressed steel side rails and cross members with solid axles supported by semi-elliptic springs front and rear. Later models of the RL became the first Alfa Romeos to use four wheel brakes and friction shock absorbers.

The motor, a completely new design from the Portello factory, was Merosi's tour de force. It was an in line six-cylinder using a one piece cast iron cylinder block with separate crankcase and sump castings. The detachable cast iron head incorporated pushrod operated overhead valves. From a displacement of 2916 cc, it developed 56 hp at 3200 rpm. The ignition was still by magneto with the mixture being fed through a single updraft carburetor. Power was transmitted through a four speed transmission and fed through an open drive-shaft to a live rear axle. Following a trend that was becoming popular in the post World War I years, Alfa used 19 in. wire wheels and twelve volt electrics for lighting and starting.

This new model was built during a period of difficult economic times in the industrial history of Italy. Luckily, Alfa had a gem of a car on its hands, and the RL revitalized the marque of the serpent during this rough period and helped it to stay afloat. The RL was officially unveiled to both critical and public acclaim in Milan on October 13, 1921, with the London introduction following afterwards.

By 1922, two versions were in production, the RL Normale and the RL Sport. The RL Sport featured a 1 cm increase in bore giving a displacement placement of 2994 cc. With the larger displacement, two single barrel updraft carburetors and larger valves, the RL Sport motor put out 71 hp, a 27 percent increase over the RL Normale! Both versions of the RL were extremely successful both commercially and on the track through 1927 when Alfa discontinued production in favor of the 6C 1500

In those five years, the Portello factory produced 1,315 Normales, 387 of the 61-hp

Turismos, 537 Sports, and 392 of the 83-hp Super Sports, for a grand total of 2,631 series production RLs.

The ultimate expression of the RL was the RL Targa Florio, which was built in 1923 and 1924. Designed especially for racing, the RL Targa Florios featured seven main bearings, a shortened chassis, and light weight two seat bodywork. Total production consisted of four 2994-cc models, two 3154-cc models, and two 3620-cc models. The 3620-cc RLs put out 125 hp at 3800 rpm—good for a top speed of 180 kmph!

The RL's parts came from many different manufacturers, all of which contributed to its elegance and handling, helping to make it a commercial success. The Sport version in particular was very popular, especially after Merosi shortened the wheelbase by 30 cm and equipped the motor with a dry sump. With a dry weight of 1750 kg, the RL Sport could easily zip along at 130 kmph, a staggering speed when you consider the state of the roads in 1920s Italy. The RL was far more powerful than most of its contemporaries on the road, adding

to the danger of driving it since its driver would, of course, want to pass everyone else.

For RL's third series in September 1923, Alfa replaced the earlier external contracting brake bands with brake shoes operating on the internal surfaces of the drums. More importantly, however, front wheel brakes were added as well, making stopping a much easier task. It didn't take long for the RL Sport and the RL Super Sport to achieve a reputation as unbeatable. In the world of racing at the time, there was simply no rival. A new generation of drivers, including Ugo Sivocci, Antonio Ascari, Giuseppe Campari, and Louis Wagner took the helm of the RL. The driver to become most famous was Enzo Ferrari who went on to win many victories for Alfa Romeo both as a driver and a team manager.

Speed wasn't the only alluring quality of the RL as high society embraced this new model Alfa as well. Many crowned heads and famous politicians couldn't resist the intoxication of

traveling long distances or even simply cruising around the piazza in an Alfa Romeo RL.

The model reproduced in these pages is a 1924 RL bodied by Carrozzeria Falco of Milan. In the 1920s, it was driven by Vittorio Ascari, brother of the famous driver Antonio Ascari, and founder of Carrozzeria Touring in 1926, the successor to Carrozzeria Falco. This particular car was then owned by a Sicilian gentleman and forgotten for many years. It has been restored it to its original splendor by its newest owner, a passionate collector.

P2: ONWARDS TO INTERNATIONAL FAME

One day in September of 1923, Enzo Ferrari went to Via San Massimo in Turin, Italy, to visit the Fiat technician, Vittorio Jano. He hoped to convince the young engineer to move to Milan to work at the nearby Portello works. Luckily for Ferrari and the future of Alfa, Jano agreed. As soon as Nicola Romeo laid eyes on the young Piemontese designer, he gave Jano the task of designing a car that could compete with the Fiat 804/404 and the Fiat 805/405, the two cars which dominated the racetracks of Europe. Since Jano knew the workings of Fiat, Romeo thought that he could design a new Grand Prix car that could challenge them. This was the birth of Jano's P2.

Thrilled to have this new designer, Alfa Romeo created a new technical office for Jano, enabling the P2 to be finished in the short period of five months. By March 1924 the engine was ready and by June 2, the not-yet-painted, two-seat body was photographed for the first time. The body was low, long, and slim with a lengthy hood that housed the powerful eight-cylinder dual overhead cam supercharged engine.

This prototype was taken out onto the racetrack and subjected to brutal treatment from Antonio Ascari and Giuseppe Campari—showing the great potential of the car. The car was ready following brief break-in sessions at Monza and on the tortuous climb from Parma to Poggia di Berceto. On June 9, the P2 debuted at the 200 Miglia di Cremona, winning the day and reaching the amazing speed of 195 kmph. Needless to say, the P2 was a success.

Vittorio Jano had designed a truly outstanding automobile. The P2's 1987 cc (61x85 mm) straight eight motor was built up of four sets of two light steel cylinders with welded-on ports and water jacketing. The crankshaft was constructed in two pieces, the dual overhead camshafts were gear driven, and the mixture was fed through an Alfa produced Roots style supercharger from an updraft Memini carburetor. Just before the Italian Grand Prix in October 1924, the sin-

On top:
Campari and
Marinoni in a P2.
Above:
Campari taking a turn at
the Lione racetrack in a P2
during the second Grand
Prix of Europe in 1924.
This car was an extraordinary success on the track.

gle carburetor was replaced with double Memini carburetors. On the first series of the car in 1924 the engine's compression was 6:1, which produced 140 hp at 5500 rpm. The engine's power was raised to 155 hp in 1925 and to 175 hp in 1930.

While the engine may have been a new design, the chassis was more conventional, using stamped steel side rails and crossmembers, with semi-elliptic springs supporting solid axles front and rear. Like the Alfa RL, the P2 also had mechanical brakes on all four wheels for quicker stopping. The

25

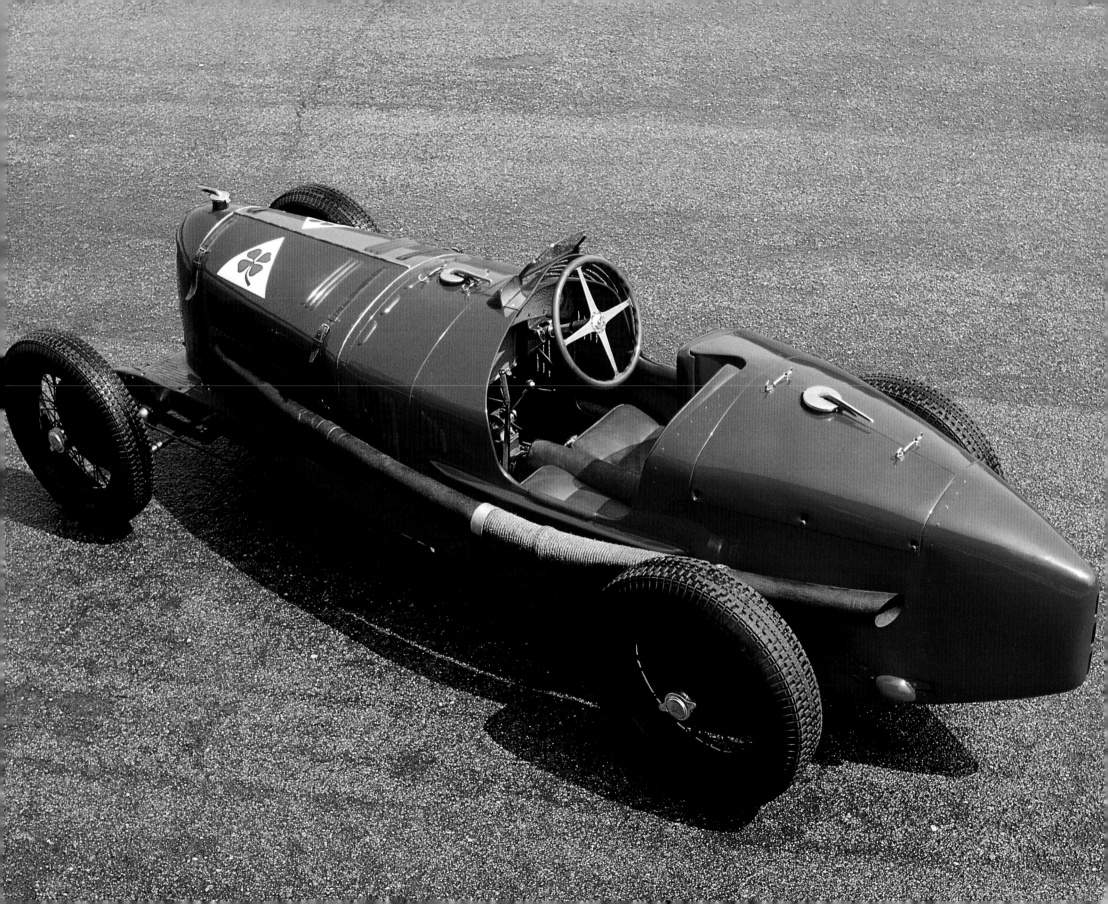

gearbox was the standard four speed unit, this time driving the rear axle through a torque tube. An unusual feature of the P2 was the position of the rear springs, which were mounted on the inside of the frame rails and tapered inwards at the rear of the car as seen from above.

The P2 appeared at its first international race on August 3, 1924, at the Grand Prix of Europe at the Lione racetrack. With all the speedy competition lined up on the 23 km track, the newest Alfa Romeo demonstrated its superiority in the seven hour race with Giuseppe Campari driving to victory and Louis Wagner placing fourth, with Antonio Ascari retiring on the last lap. From that day forward, Jano's new masterpiece was legendary on the street and the racetrack.

In 1924 and 1925, Antonio Ascari, Giuseppe Campari, Louis Wagner, and Gastone Brilli-Peri all had victories behind the wheel of the P2. In 1925, this extraordinary car won its first World Championship, an award that had just begun that year. In honor of this success, a laurel wreath was added to the radiator badge of every Alfa.

The P2 went on to dominate the "Formula Libera" class and achieved numerous victories in both circuit and road racing. The "Golden Book" of racing victories for the unbeatable Alfa Romeo shows 18 victories and 20 placements between 1924 and 1930.

Of the six P2s built at Portello, two are still in existence. The example photographed in these pages is now in the Alfa Romeo Museo Storico at Arese and has never been restored. This beautiful P2 is a testament to the unforgettable pages of racing history written by the House of Portello.

8C 2300 MONZA: FROM THE GOLDEN AGE OF ALFAS

After leaving the official racing team of Alfa Romeo, Enzo Ferrari established his own racing team in Modena on December 1, 1929. At first, Ferrari's goal was simply to help independent drivers compete behind the wheel of the car from the marque of the serpent. Only later did he once again head up the factory racing team for the famous Alfa Romeo of Milan. From the dawn of 1933 until the beginning of the second World War, it was up to Enzo Ferrari to keep the Alfa banner flying high.

By the end of the 1920s, Alfa held a position of international prestige. It ruled innumerable international road competitions with its beautiful automobiles with the P2 being invincible in Grand Prix racing.

People were on the edge of their seats waiting for the next car designed by Vittorio Jano, in hopes that it could compare with the feared Bugatti. At the beginning of 1931 this amazing technician from Turin unveiled the 8C 2300. With a super-charged straight eight engine, it was derived from the P2, but with a far more sophisticated and innovative level of planning and execution.

The motor consisted of two light alloy cylinder blocks fitted with steel liners and aluminum pis-

tons. The crankcase, sump, and two detachable cylinder heads were also cast of light alloy. The dual overhead camshafts were driven by a gear train residing between the two cylinder blocks. Although the crankshaft was built in two parts like that of the P2, it did not run in roller bearings, but rather in ten babbit lined bronze bearings. The bore and stroke were identical to that of the 6C 1750 motor, for a displacement of 2336 cc (65x88 mm); with a Roots compressor and a compression ratio of 5.75:1, the new eight-cylinder Portello motor delivered 142 hp at 5000 rpm.

While the engine was very innovative, the rest of the chassis was strictly conventional. The front and rear had rigid axles with semi-elliptical leaf springs while friction shock absorbers and mechanically-controlled brakes were used on all four wheels. The Monza was available in two wheelbases, lungo and corto. The Monza model, shown on these pages is the corto version. The wheelbase is 265 cm, 10 cm shorter than the production model. Compared to its predecessor, the 8C 2300, the Monza delivered greater power (165 hp at 5400 rpm) and put two shock absorbers on the rear for a more controlled ride. With a dry weight of 920 kg, the car could achieve the highly acclaimed top speed of 210 kmph.

The Monza debuted at the 1931 Gran Premio d'Italia where Tazio Nuvolari and Giuseppe Campari traded off driving during ten hard hours of racing. While the checkered flag waved them to a sensational victory; the Minoia/Borzacchini team was a nose behind them in another 8C 2300 Monza.

For the 1932 season of racing, Alfa Romeo entrusted its reputation to the brand new single-seat P3, while Scuderia Ferrari stuck with the tried and true Monza. The Monza dominated the track with such drivers as Tazio Nuvolari and Rudolf Caracciola in the first two positions at the Gran Prix de Monaco, with Nuvolari winning the Targa Florio. The Monza went on to repeat its victory at the Targa Florio in 1933

with Antonio Brivio at the wheel. In the Sport category, the Monza was outfitted with fenders and headlights, but basically did not change significantly from the Grand Prix version.

At the beginning of 1933, Alfa Romeo withdrew from competition while Scuderia Ferrari fielded the trusty 8C 2300 again at Monza, but not without first making some serious modifications. He increased the displacement to 2556 cc, upping the power to 178 hp at 5400 rpm and increasing maximum speed to 225 kmph. In 1934, Scuderia Ferrari entered four of these cars in the eighth Mille Miglia and the one driven by the team of Varzi/Bignami took another historic triumph.

Alfa only produced ten examples of the 8C 2300 Monza, six in 1931 and four the year after. Of these, only one has survived to be partially restored in 1975; it now sits in the Museo Storico in Arese.

6C 1500 N: A NEW LINE OF ALFAS

By the end of the summer in 1924, the P2 had transformed Alfa Romeo into the rising star of car companies. In spite of its many victories on the racetrack, Alfa's success was more a matter of luck than company strategy. While the Super Sport and Targa Florio versions of the RL had some amazing successes, the P1's race at the Grand Prix of 1923 could hardly be compared to the competition. On top of the mediocre performance of the P1,

the RM model, which came out in 1923 with a two liter, four-cylinder engine, had only a fair showing on the market.

The superb trial runs by the P2, however, confirmed to the world that Alfa meant quality: quality in the form of the extraordinary design of Vittorio Jano and the high level of mechanical work and assembly of parts at the Portello works. So why not transfer this engineering and production

expertise onto a medium capacity automobile that could make the marque of the serpent a commercial fortune? Jano, of course, was entrusted with this new project. He envisioned yet another new engine design of a liter and a half capacity mounted in a light chassis with good brakes. The car, initially dubbed the NR 1500, became the 6C 1500 Normale.

The six cylinder 1487 cc (62x82 mm) motor featured a cast iron cylinder block and head with cast light alloy crankcase and finned sump. The single overhead camshaft was driven by a vertical shaft mounted at the rear of the motor. The mixture was fed through a two barrel updraft Zenith carburetor. With a compression ratio of 5.75:1, the motor produced 44 hp at 4200 rpm. The transmission, once again, was the classic four speed followed by torque tube drive to the solid rear axle. The car was equipped with semi-elliptical springs, friction shocks, and both pedal and hand-controlled mechanical brakes on all four wheels. The two different versions of the car had different wheelbases; one measured 290 cm and the other 310 cm. With a dry weight between 1000 and 1100 kg, the 1500 Normale could reach a top speed of 110 kmph.

At the Salone dell'Auto of Milan in April 1925, the chassis was shown without the body. Following this debut, it was later

exhibited in Paris and London. Compared to the other factories' exhibits, it was one of the most innovative projects at the shows. The high rpm engine, the flexibility of the frame combined with the rigid springs, the highly efficient brakes, and its relatively light weight made for exquisite handling that was almost unknown even for luxury cars of the time. The 6C 1500 was delivered to buyers in the spring of 1927, but by 1928 a second series of this model was already in production. Production continued until 1929 with a total of 862 units of the 6C 1500 Normale manufactured by the Portello works.

The 6C 1500 N also had a brief but intense life on the racetrack. It debuted on June 5, 1927, at Modena where Enzo Ferrari, that young concessionaire of the marque, drove the 6C 1500 to victory. A year later, a Sport version with a 54-hp twin cam engine ran its first race. In addition to the Sport, three versions of the Super Sport were produced: the first produced 60 hp, the second had a supercharged motor producing 76 hp, and the third, with a fixed cylinder head and supercharger gave 84 hp.

The 6C 1500 N seen on these pages is an elegant enclosed drive sedan produced in 1928. The body was made by Carrozzeria Touring, a young company which had just entered into the automobile business and would become an important partner to Alfa in the coming years.

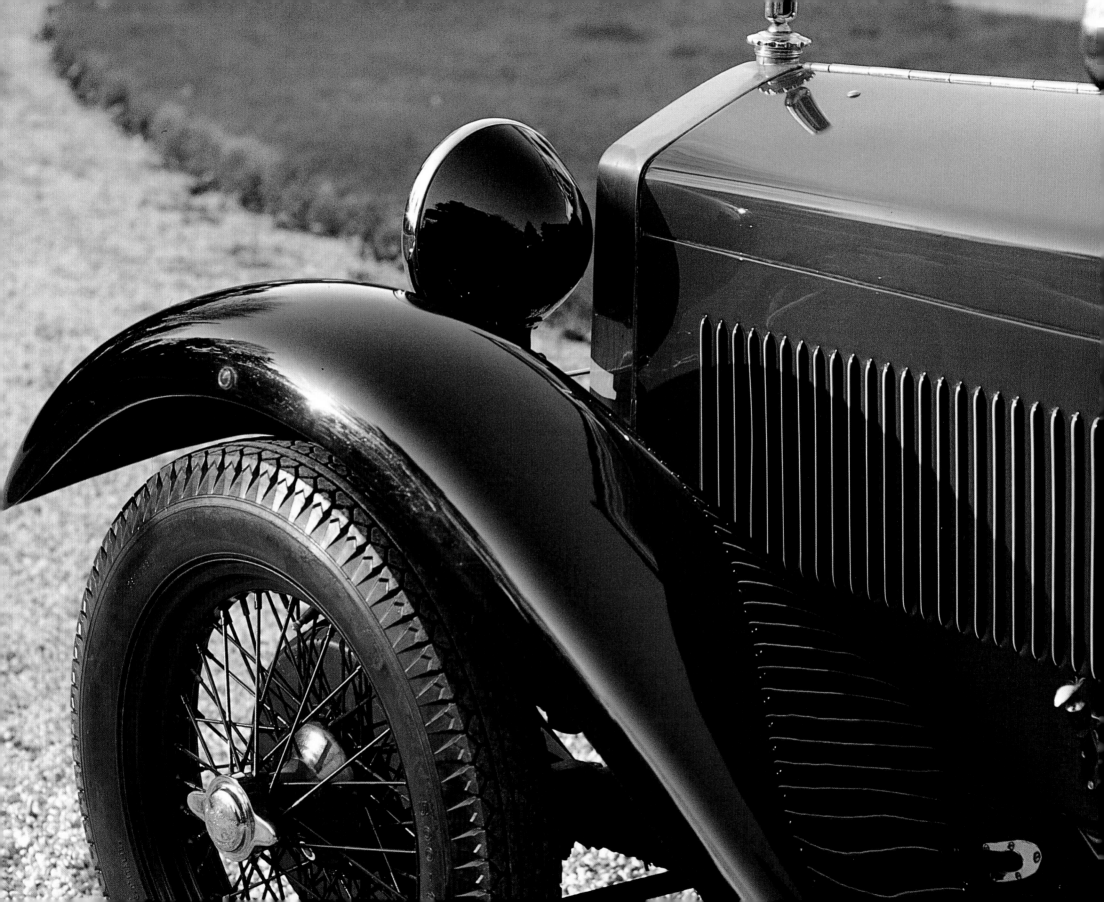

6C 1750 GT: THE TOURING KING

At the 1928 Mille Miglia, Alfa Romeo redeemed itself from the defeat of the previous year. OM had claimed its fame at the first Mille Miglia in 1927 in Brescia, Italy, by besting Alfa and the other leading auto manufacturers.

But in 1928, with Campari and Ramponi at the wheel of a supercharged 6C 1500 Super Sport, Alfa once again showed what they could do. Lancias, Bugattis, Maseratis, and OMs were left in the dust by the 1500 SS, which averaged a speed of 84 kmph during the race. It even passed another Alfa, an RL Super Sport, proving that its advanced design was truly revolutionary. The exceptional engine of the 1500 SS would influence the evolution of racing motors for years to come.

At the Portello works, Vittorio Jano was already devising the next stage of his extraordinary six-cylinder motor. By enlarging the bore and stroke by 3 mm and 6 mm respectively, bringing the displacement to 1752 cc (65x88 mm), and feeding the mixture through a double throat Zenith carburetor, he achieved 46 hp at 4000 rpm.

This was how the 6C 1750 model had its origin; it is a direct descendant of the 6C 1500 of 1927. The car was officially presented in Rome in February of 1929, at the Salone dell'Automobile, during the one time in which the exhibition appeared in the Italian capital. The new engine came in two versions: the single cam, which was previewed as the Turismo model, and the twin cam available in the Sport model of the third series in 1929, and later renamed the Gran Turismo in the fourth and fifth series of 1930 to 1932. On the twin cam motor, the compression ratio was raised from 5.5:1 to 5.75:1, giving a maximum power output of 55 hp at 4400 rpm.

The new Alfa Romeo embodied the spirit of "granturismo," as we've come to know it today, that is, it was light, agile, and manageable, with good brakes. It easily reached 125 kmph, with reliable and simple mechanics. The chassis sported a similar design to that of the 6C 1500, with slight modifications and some strengthening. The Turismo model of 1929 had 29x5.25 tires on 18 inch wheels, while the Sport and Gran Turismo versions had 28x5.50 tires on 17 inch wheels.

The 6C 1750 GT remained almost unchanged during its four years of production. 268 of the series 3 were produced, followed by 652 more of the series 4 and 5. The last two series were equipped with an adjustable regulating device which allowed the intake mixture to be heated by the exhaust manifold.

With a wheelbase of 292 cm (exactly the same as the 6C 1500 S and SS), this new model

could accommodate a spider, torpedo, or berlina bodywork. Starting between 1930 and 1931 the Portello factory also began building its own bodies, limiting itself initially to the production of all metal four- and six-window berlinas.

On the racing front, the 6C 1750 GT wasn't a key player. The Super Sport and Gran Sport dominated the racetrack with their much greater power and speed. But on the highways, to pass a Gran Turismo was always considered a difficult task, since the car possessed a rare combination of acceleration, agility, handling, and good braking.

The photographs on these pages show a beautiful four-seater cabriolet produced by Ugo Zagato in 1930. It is unmistakable, with the smooth and harmonious lines that the Milanese carrozzeria applied not only to its spider, but also to its cars with a less sporting calling. The attentive reader shouldn't miss the Zagato coachbuilder's plate with silver letters on a black background. This became the carrozzeria's signature after the victory of the Zagato bodied Alfa Romeo in the 1928 Mille Miglia.

6C 1750 GS: ON THE WINGS OF A LEGEND

Below:
Lord Howe with his 1750
at Le Mans where he
placed fifth in 1930.
Bottom:
Nuvolari and Guidotti in
Florence during the 1930
Mille Miglia.

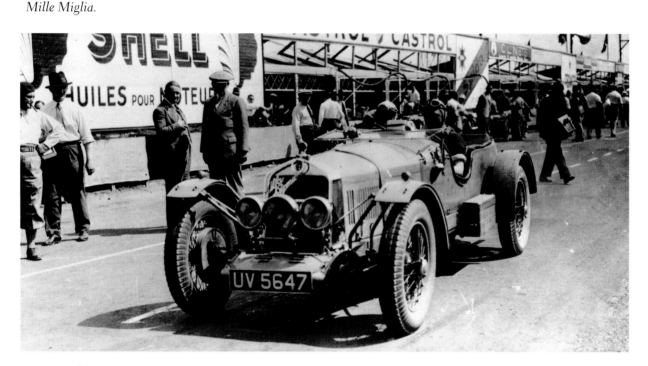

T he Gran Sport is the most beautiful and prestigious of the 6C 1750 models and is the one that helped shape the legend of Alfa Romeo in the third decade of this century. It was renamed as such in 1930 to distinguish it from the previous year's Super Sport which had a supercharged engine. The original plans of the six-cylinder engine of Vittorio Jano revealed that it was capable of brilliant developments: the dual overhead camshafts, a Roots supercharger with two lobes, not to mention a dual throat Memini horizontal carburetor, all on a 1752-cc engine with a 65x88 mm bore and stroke delivering 85 hp at 4500 rpm.

The chassis was tuned as well; in particular, the wheelbase was reduced from 292 cm on the GT model to 274 cm on the Sport version. This radically changed the handling of the car; it was now extraordinarily agile and could be controlled more easily under severe conditions. As the chassis and balance of the car changed, so too, did its personality. This allowed some carrozzerias to create miracles, in particular, Zagato with the 1930 two-seat aluminum bodied spider seen on these pages.

Conceived primarily for competition, the 6C 1750 GS dominated contemporary racing with its enthusiastic performance, made extra special by its structural simplicity and its mechanical trustworthiness. Among its winning characteristics was the exceptional readiness of its motor, providing rapid and smooth progression all the way to the rev limit.. The

suspension settings were rigid but not hard, due to the exceptional length of the springs and the correct firmness of the shock absorbers. This allowed the car to be driven with great ease. The wheel could be controlled with the fingers, leaving the car to follow the desired course. It possessed the rare characteristic of being docile and aggressive at the same time. With a dry weight of 920 kg, the Gran Sport could cruise at a top speed of 145 kmph, an exceptional speed for a car of 1930 with under two liters of displacement.

The sporting newspapers recorded the triumphs of the Gran Sport in every type of racing. While still wearing the SS logo, it made its debut in the 1929 Mille Miglia, with a victory by the Campari/Ramponi team. For the most difficult races, Alfa prepared six official

cars in 1929 and another six in 1930. The diameter of the intake valves was enlarged from 28 mm to 30 mm, with the inclination changing from 90 degrees to 100 degrees. In the 1929 version, the maximum power was 85 hp at 4800 rpm but in 1930 this was raised to 102 hp at 5000 rpm. With the dry weight reduced to 840 kg, the 1930 Gran Sport could reach 170 kmph.

In 1929, the 1750 had a long series of successes all over Europe: at the Twenty-four Hours of Spa, at the Twelve Hours of San Sebastian, at the Irish Grand Prix and in Belgium. The 1750 conquered national races as well, at the Coppa della Consuma and at Trieste-Opicina. In 1930, the four official Gran Sports for the Alfa Romeo team at the Mille Miglia were the top four placers, with Tazio Nuvolari winning with an average speed of more than 100 kmph! During the same year, the formidable car placed in the top three at the Twenty-four Hours of Spa and the Tourist Trophy. Then came a myriad of other successes and record-breaking World Cups, including records set at Montlhery both for 4,000 miles and 48 hours, where they maintained an average speed of more than 151 kmph.

Only 257 examples of the 6C 1750 GS were produced from 1930 to 1933, in the fourth, fifth, and sixth series. Because of its rarity, it is definitely one of the most collectable Alfas. The Gran Sport was a glorious representative of its time and even today it is fascinating as a timeless thoroughbred.

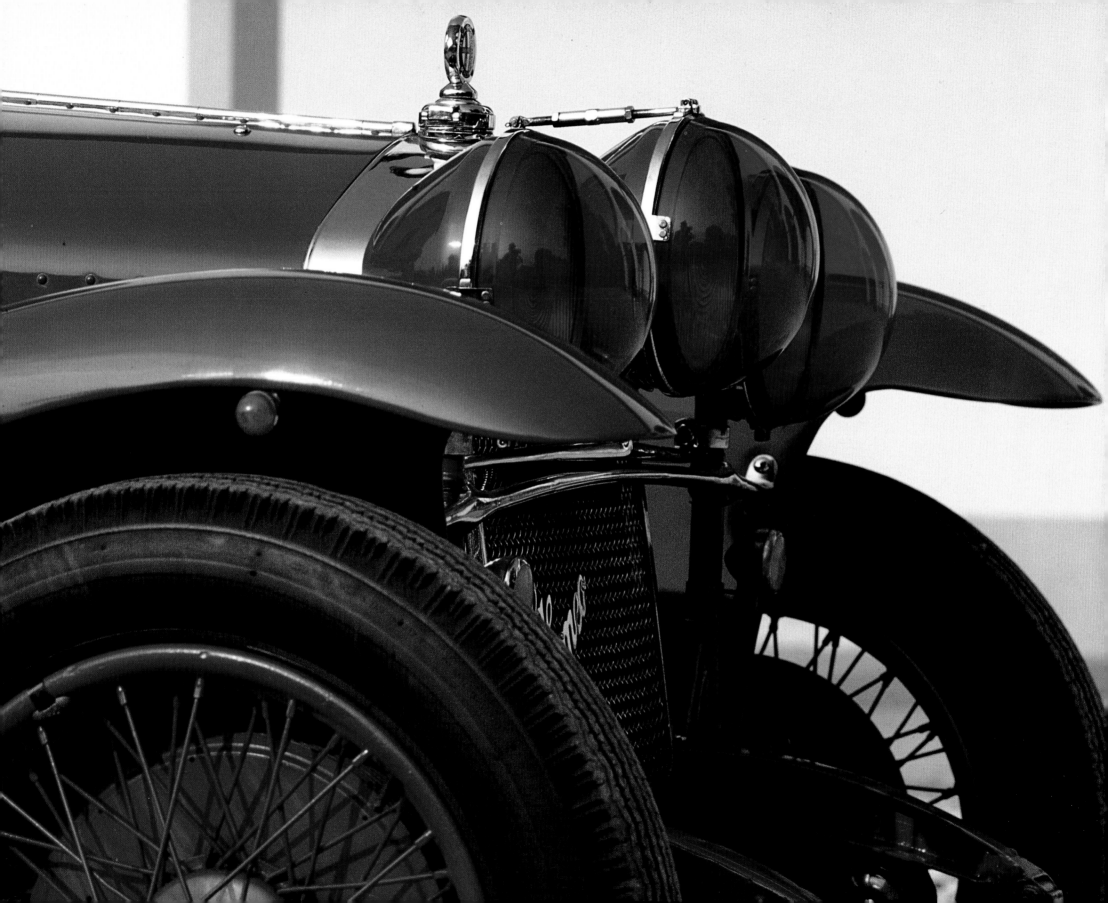

6C 1750 GTC: DIRECT FROM THE RACETRACK

In 1931 the 6C 1750 model was at the top in the competitive field and had acquired fame with an exclusive group of international clients. Alfa Romeo decided to extend the line with the Gran Turismo Compressore, destined to satisfy the aspirations of its numerous customers who were looking for a comfortable car with the high prestige of Portello's irresistible supercharged motor. The mechanicals of the 1750 Super Sport and Gran

Sport, tested with complete success in hundreds of races, were now ready to enter the luxury sports market with the introduction of a new generation of Alfa whose berlina and torpedo bodies gave it noticeably sporting lines.

The six cylinder motor kept the 1752-cc (65x88 mm) displacement, 5:1 compression ratio, dual overhead camshafts, twin choke Memini side-draft carburetor, and Roots supercharger. The camshaft drive was the same as used on the 1929 Gran Turismo, instead of the that of the Gran Sport. Overall, the engine was slightly detuned to produce 80 hp instead of the 85 hp of the Sport and Grand Sport.

More modifications were made to the chassis and the transmission. The wheelbase of the car was increased to 316 cm in order to accommodate the more luxurious bodies, the new 8C 2300 derived front axle and transmission were used and the shock absorbers were now adjustable directly from the drivers seat. To safely deal with the increased weight of 1360 kg (including the two spare wheels), the diameter of the front brake drums was increased from 320 mm to 400 mm. Additionally, the tire size

the carrozzerias of Touring, Castagna, Cesare Sala, Garavini, and Zagato. Abroad, chiefly in Great Britain, the work of these carrozzerias revitalized enthusiasm for Alfa amongst both the public and the motoring press. The new 6C 1750 GTC was following in the footsteps of the already famous earlier Alfa Romeo 6Cs.

The GTC Torpedo Gran Sport on these pages is part of an Italian collection preserved in excellent condition—a testament to the master craftsmen at Carrozzeria Castagna. This completely original double phaeton four-seater was produced in 1931 with the chassis number 101014804, the fourth 6C 1750 GTC chassis produced at Portello. The whole of the agile and dynamic design is emphasized by the curved lines beginning at the top of the radiator, flowing back over the hood and descending to follow the waist line. The ventilation louvers on the sides of the hood, cowl, and running board valences and the cut down front doors are not only functional but add to the overall beauty of the design.

The 1750 GTC's existence was short-lived, and its production was only part of the fifth series of the 6C in the years 1931 to 1932. In total, only 159 of the 1750 GTC were built at the Portello works, but in each one of them could be found the qualities which exemplified the greatness of the 1750 family.

was increased to 30x6 in place of the 28x5.5 used on the Gran Turismo and the 27x4.75 on the 1929 Super Sport. The new 6C 1750 GTC could reach a maximum speed of 135 kmph, no mean feat for a small displacement four passenger luxury automobile.

Thanks to the greater width and the practical extension of the hood (able to house the motor and the supercharger), the already great 1750 of Vittorio Jano had a new look which was even more slender and stately than before. Apart from the berlina and berlinetta versions produced at Portello, some of the best Italian body makers created GTC bodies: masterworks came from

6C 1900 GT: THE EVOLUTION OF A SPECIES

In spite of 1931 being a rich year for new cars, it was a year of turmoil for many Italian car manufacturers. Auto production survived in spite of the large drop in the overall number of cars produced: 25,800 cars total, a level which hadn't been seen since right after World War I. At Alfa Romeo, 492 units were produced, of which 468 were in the 6C series. In 1932 Portello offered four different models of the 6C 1750: the Turismo, the Gran Turismo, the Gran Sport, and the Gran Turismo Compressore, in addition to the brand-new 8C 2300. Despite only 24 cars being produced, the 8C 2300 Became a key player in a triumphant season on the racetrack. Production for 1932 rose to 582 cars with the most popular being the 6C 1750 Turismo, It was the least expensive with the least sophisticated motor but was the easiest to use for most drivers. 8C 2300 production increased to 68 cars.

At the 1933 Salone dell'Automobile in Milan, the marque of the serpent presented the 1900 GT, which evolved separately from the 6C series. By means of enlarging the bore by 3 mm, the size of Vittorio Jano's engine was increased to 1917 cc (68x88 mm). The cast iron

cylinder head was replaced with one cast in aluminum alloy, with other structural improvements to the motor being new connecting rods and pistons. With a compression ratio of 6.25:1 and an updraft two-barrel Solex carburetor (fed by an electric fuel pump!) the non-supercharged motor put out 68 hp at 4500 rpm.

The gearbox was, as usual, a four-speed with reverse, but it underwent some modifications with the introduction of third and fourth gear synchromesh and a "free wheel" device that helped save engine wear. The frame was completely redesigned, and was reinforced in the front (as was that of the 6C 1750 GTC), the springs were now anchored to the frame with rubber bushings which helped to further smooth the ride.

With the same 292 cm wheelbase as the 6C 1750 Gran Turismo and with the track slightly increased from 138 cm to 142 cm, the 6C 1900 Gran Turismo had a dry weight of 1250 kg in the four-door berlina version. Its maximum speed was 130 kmph, which was consistent with the other Alfas in this series. It was considered a touring model, with speed

adequate for the rapidly improving Italian roads of the time.

A large part of the 1900 GT's chassis was produced at Portello, including the entire drive train and the internal metal structure. These parts were characterized by a style which was typical of the time period, but certainly devoid of many of the fancy curves and flourishes favored by many of the design houses of the era. It was, however, a car that played an important role in the process of production innovation at the beginning of the 1930s.

The artisans of the various carrozzerias didn't give up on clothing the mechanicals of the 6C 1900 GT. At the 6C 1900 GT's introduction at the Salone dell'Automobile in Milan, Touring presented a berlina while at the same time, Castagna presented both a berlina and a cabriolet.

A Touring cabriolet, a Farina berlina, and other bodies by Castagna (like the cabriolet pictured on these pages) saw the light of day in 1933. In that same year, with a total production of 197, the end came for the 6C 1900 Gran Turismo as Alfa ceased production of the sixth series 6C in favor of the 6C 2300.

6C 2300 B GT: THE DAWN OF A NEW BEGINNING

At the Salone dell'-Automobile of Milan in 1934, Alfa Romeo presented the 6C 2300 model, the seventh series in the long line of 6Cs beginning with the 1500. The 6C 2300 was considered to be an entirely new car by the Portello works however. Jano redesigned the in-line six-cylinder engine especially for the 6C 2300. For the first time at Alfa,

the crankcase and cylinders were combined in a one piece iron casting. The cylinder head was, as in the 6C 1900, a one piece aluminum casting with provision for dual overhead camshafts. With a displacement of 2309 cc (70x100 mm), an updraft two-barrel Solex carburetor, and a compression ratio of 6.5:1 the new engine developed 68 hp at 4400 rpm.

One year later, the 6C 2300 was mechanically modified to such an extent that a "B" was added to its official name. This was the beginning a new generation of cars; the first series was in 1935 and continued through 1939. The Gran Turismo and the Pescara models were the most popular cars in this series, which continued to demonstrate that Alfa's specialty was seen as sports cars.

Except for the six-cylinder motor of 2309 cc (70x100 mm) which debuted the year before on the racetrack with a brilliant triumph, the Alfa 2300 of 1935 presented an automobile with an entirely new concept: the four wheels had independent suspension and hydraulic brakes. The front suspension was a direct descendant of that used on the single-seat P3 (which had been introduced for racing in 1935). The semi-elliptic front springs were abandoned in favor of a Dubonnet system. This consisted of two longitudinal trail-

ing arms which carried the front stub axles with an additional lateral arm acting on a combined coil spring/hydraulic shock absorber unit. The independent rear suspension consisted of swing axles located by trailing arms coupled to longitudinal torsion bars and telescopic shock absorbers.

Along with the solid axles, the mechanical brakes were also abandoned with the introduction of the 6C 2300 B, for by the 1930s, other manufacturers were already using hydraulic brakes on various models of cars. The new hydraulic system eliminated the necessity of frequent adjustment of the brake connecting rods and above all made the front brakes completely separate from the steering. The transmission of the 2300 B also underwent many modifications; with constant-mesh second, third, and fourth gears and syncromesh on third and fourth. Three new flexible couplings replaced universal joints on the drive shaft, while the differential housing was attached to the frame with rubber mounts for maximum isolation.

The Gran Turismo version had a 76 hp motor. It went into production with a wheelbase of 300 cm, and a track measuring 144 cm at the front and 146 cm at the rear (which was a slight increase from the 6C 2300 of 1934). The berlina body was built at Portello and had a certain stylishness with its teardrop shaped front and rear fenders. With a dry weight of 1380 kg, the 6C 2300 B GT could reach 130 kmph, which was the fastest of any other berlinas series built during that period of Italian history. Only 16

cars were built during its first year of production—one of which survived and is photographed on these pages. Due to military production commitments, no 6C 2300 B GT's were built in 1936. That year Alfa's yearly automotive production reached an all time low with only five 6C 2300 B Pescaras and five 8C 2900 A's being manufactured. Production of the 6C 2300 B GT resumed in 1937 with 70 being produced before the first series was superseded by the second series in 1938.

More popular was the Pescara version with a 95 hp motor and coachwork primarily by Touring who produced the attractive ultra light berlinetta featured on these pages. While some chassis were bodied by other specialists, these were generally of a more conservative design and were not destined to stand out in competition. Between 1935 and 1937, 120 of the 6C 2300 B Pescara models were sold to customers.

6C 2300 B MILLE MIGLIA: LEADER OF THE PACK

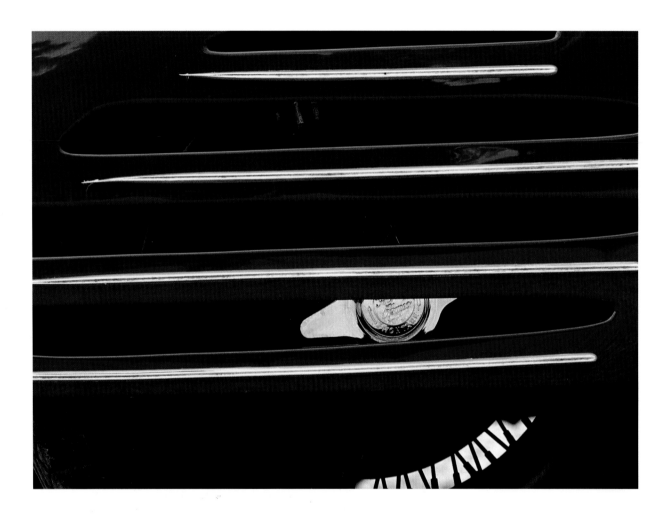

only take modest advantage of this new wave of popularity for, in those years, it had to pool its resources towards making trucks and airplane engines for the Italian military build-up.

On the other hand, the huge number of racing victories, including the Mille Miglia and other important European races, stimulated technical research towards the development of better engines. Carrozzeria Touring, meanwhile, was working with Alfa on the creation of a fast berlinetta with an improved power to weight ratio.

From these beginnings the 6C 2300 B Mille Miglia came to life at the beginning of 1937. This car was very important for the Milanese company because it was the first of the "Superleggera" (superlight) line. At Touring it was realized that the lightweight Weymann system of body construction—a wooden framework covered with imitation leather—could be improved upon through the use of a framework of small diameter steel tubing covered by an aluminum skin.

Apart from a significant weight reduction and an improvement in the rigidity of the car

The incredible success of the Alfa 2300 Pescara on the racetrack in 1934 and the two following years, created new interest in the series of non-supercharged Alfa Romeos. The Portello works, however, could

as a whole, the "Superleggera" method of body construction allowed the designers much greater stylistic freedom. They could now create ever more curvaceous and aerodynamic lines. The bodywork on the Mille Miglia berlinetta—with its streamlined rear fenders integrated into the body and roof tapering sharply to the rear—heavily influenced the style of future Touring designs. The bodywork's weight was exceptionally low, a mere 126 kg, thanks in part to the introduction of redesigned seats and Plexiglas for the side and rear windows.

Beneath the bodywork, the mechanics at Alfa did their part to improve the 6C 2300 B Pescara. With a compression ratio of 7.75:1 and using two side-draft single choke Solex carburetors, the Mille Miglia developed 105 hp at 4800 rpm. The experimental berlinetta, with three seats and a dry weight of 1150 kg, could reach 170 kmph. Testing its incredible potential for the first time in the Mille Miglia on April 5, 1937 was chief test driver, Giovanbattista Guidotti with Ercole Boratto (the personal driver of Benito Mussolini) in the

passenger seat. They finished fourth overall, and first in the over 1500 cc Turismo class. In December of the same year, the Alfa Romeo berlinetta won the first Bengasi-Tripoli race, this time with Boratto at the wheel. It completed the 1020 km race at the astonishing average speed of 134 kmph.

In 1938, Alfa Romeo decided to put the Mille Miglia berlinetta into production as the second series of the 2300 B. The auto represented all the great qualities of its racing prototype: the powerful engine, producing 105 hp at 4800 rpm, the exquisite lightweight aluminum bodywork, and all the rest of the outstanding design. A total of 107 of these cars were produced, one of which is pictured on these pages; this car is kept in excellent condition in a private collection in Italy.

8C 2900 B AERODINAMICA: THE SHATTERED DREAM OF LE MANS

In 1935 Vittorio Jano created a small series of high performance luxury sports cars using engines developed for the single-seat type B Grand Prix cars. While the straight eight cylinder motors had become outclassed by the Germans on the race track, they were ideal for what would become the definitive performance car of its era. Not only was the 8C 2900 the fastest car on the road in the late 1930s, it was also the most sophisticated, expensive, and elegant automobile that the Portello works had ever offered for sale.

In effect, the various components found on the majestic spider which debuted at the 1935 Salon de l'Automobile de Paris were found on other Alfa models of the time. It was the combination of these various elements on this one model that made the total far greater than the sum of its parts. Few other car manufacturers of the time were able to achieve this level of excellence.

The mechanicals of the 8C 2900 A were remarkable, being very similar to the P3. The motor, for example, was made up of a single piece crankcase topped by two sets of cylinder blocks with fixed heads and steel liners with all castings in light alloy. The valve train consisted of dual overhead cams driven, as in the earlier Alfa straight eights, by a gear train mounted centrally between the cylinder blocks. The fuel system consisted of two electric fuel pumps, two updraft Weber carbure-

tors, and two Roots style superchargers while lubrication was provided by a dry sump system incorporating two mechanical oil pumps. With a displacement of 2905 cc (68x100 mm) and a compression ratio of 6.5:1, the motor developed 220 hp at 5300 rpm. The rear-mounted four-speed transaxle came from the Tipo C grand prix cars of 1935 and 1936. The rear independent suspension incorporated swing axles, trailing arms, a transverse leaf spring, and two telescopic and two adjustable friction shock absorbers. The front suspension was by the same Dubonnet system used on the 6C 2300 B Pescara. The hydraulic brakes featured large aluminum/copper alloy drums with ferrous liners similar to the ones fitted to the 8C 2300 and Tipo B.

The 8C 2900 A debuted in the tenth Mille Miglia in 1936, where the three Scuderia Ferrari cars placed one, two, three in the general classification, with Antonio Brivio, Nino Farina, and Carlo Pintacuda driving. The next year the Portello works introduced the 8C 2900 B series, which had horsepower reduced to 180 hp, and was available in a Corto and Lungo version with wheelbases of 280 cm and 300 cm respectively. The 33 cars of this last model produced between 1937 and 1939 made their mark in racing history.

By 1938, the 8C 2900 B was set to participate in the 24 Hours of Le Mans.

The motor was bored to 2926 cc (68.25x100 mm), and with a compression ratio of 6.25:1 was now rated at 220 hp at 5500 rpm. Carrozzeria Touring produced a berlinetta "Superleggera" body with extremely avant-garde lines: fenders incorporated into the body of the car, a teardrop shaped greenhouse, and the rear of the body tapered to a sharp tail.

On the June, 18 1938 Alfa put its 8C 2900 B berlinetta special (s/n 412033) to the test at Le Mans. Clemente Biondetti and the Frenchman Raymond Sommer rode at the helm. The Alfa hit 220 kmph on the fastest parts of the track, and was already eleven laps ahead of the next contender when transmission failure caused its retirement. Dreams of victory vanished, and the 8C 2900 B berlinetta no. 412033 sank into a long period of undeserved oblivion.

The car pictured on these pages passed through the hands of numerous collectors until it was picked up by the Scottish Doune Museum in 1968. It remained there until 1982, at which time an English collector decided to restore the car. Four years later, Alfa Romeo acquired this car for its museum at Arese. It has finally returned home for good.

6C 2500 SS "1939": THE MARK OF ALFA CORSE

saying he wasn't given the freedom he needed to design the cars he wanted. Just a few months later, Alfa Romeo decided to officially re-enter the world of competition, and formed the Alfa Corse racing team. In so doing Alfa severed its relationship with Scuderia Ferrari, the team which had cast its invincible aura over Alfa Romeo. The technical know-how of Scuderia Ferrari was passed on to Alfa Corse through Enzo Ferrari, however, when he became the team's director under the jurisdiction of Alfa. He stayed until 1939, when he resigned to returned to Modena.

By the end of that year, Alfa finished the second series of the 2300 B and debuted the 6C 2500 with mechanicals based on the preceding model. Although the Alfa-built berlina body was totally new and very habitable, its lines weren't comparable to the most advanced styling tendencies of the day. Originally conceived as a third series of the 2300 B, the 6C 2500 was marketed in four different models: a 5 passenger Turismo and a 6/7 passenger Turismo, both on a 325 cm wheelbase, a Sport version with a wheelbase

The last months of 1937 were marked by a turbulent climate in the industrial and racing world, which provoked two large changes at Alfa Romeo. By the end of September, Vittorio Jano, the eclectic designer who had created numerous triumphs for Alfa, bitterly left the company,

of 300 cm, and a Super Sport with the wheelbase reduced to 270 cm.

The motor was the well-known in-line six cylinder engine of 1934 with a 2 mm enlargement of the bore which brought the displacement to 2443 cc (72x100 mm). Using technology tested time and again by Alfa, the foundries produced a monoblock engine of cast iron with a removable cylinder head in light alloy. The head was graced by valves set at 90 degrees opening onto hemispheric chambers. State of tune differences between the four models caused the horsepower to vary from version to version. The Turismo produced 87 hp; the Sport 95 hp; and the Super Sport, with a compression ratio of 8:1 and three twin-choke side draft Weber carburetors, 110 hp at 4800 rpm.

The transmission of the 6C 2500 was the four speed unit with syncromesh on third and fourth which had been used on 2300 B. The front and rear suspensions were also carried over with the front using the Dubonnet system and the rear featuring a frame mounted differential, swing axles, telescopic shock absorbers, trailing arms, and longitudinal tor-

sion bars. The brakes were four wheel hydraulic with a mechanical hand brake operating on the rear wheels.

The 6C 2500 Super Sport, the fastest and most prestigious in the line-up at the time, could reach a speed of 170 kmph. Because of their high performance, the first cars were delegated for use in racing by the drivers of Alfa Corse. Production was limited to 66 examples manufactured during the war years of 1939 to

1943. The bodywork was crafted by some of the best carrozzerias, including Touring of Milan. The berlinetta Superleggera of 1939, a four-seater, is pictured on these pages. Its extraordinary equilibrium, its tapered hood, smooth fenders, and the streamlined top all contribute to the splendid lines of this car. The 6C 2500 Super Sport was a testament to the great rapport between Carrozzeria Touring and the Portello works at the close of the 1930's.

512: THE AVANT GARDE WITHOUT FUTURE

*Two views of the second version
of the 512 without bodywork.
This is one of the two cars
constructed by Alfa Romeo before
W.W.II interrupted the
development of the 512.*

By the end of 1935,
it took little convincing to persuade the Alfa
Romeo management to experiment with new
technical approaches in an attempt to regain
competitiveness with the new German
Grand Prix cars.

These were years of passionate and convul-
sive activity at Alfa. They embarked on the
development of two new models to meet the
German threat: the 512 to contest the 1500 cc
blown formula, and the 162 designed for the
3000 cc blown category. At the same time, the
Portello works was facing growing demands for
military hardware as the international situation
became increasingly dangerous during 1938
and 1939. The nervousness, the hurry, and the
insufficient time for proper testing led to hasty
decisions at the factory. In such circumstances,
the two projects saw little chance for success.

With the arrival at Portello of the Spanish
engineer Wifredo Ricart, research entered a
new phase. The 162 was the first car produced. A single-seater with a 16 cylinder, 3
liter motor, the 162 was road tested in June
1940 and afterwards abandoned. A second
car, the 512, was conceived in 1939 to compete in the 1500 cc category, and gained

momentum as a courageous, avant-garde project. War production, already begun by 1940, unfortunately eclipsed this project, and the 512 never had a chance to prove itself.

On paper, the 512 possessed all the requirements of a revolutionary automobile. The motor held twelve opposing cylinders giving a total displacement of 1490 cc (54x54.2 mm). The split crankcase was cast of Elektron alloy while the detachable cylinder heads were of cast aluminum. The crankshaft was supported by six roller and two plain bearings. In a very early application of the principle, an auxiliary shaft was fitted to counter vibration.

A triple choke downdraft Weber carburetor fed through two dual chamber Roots compressors to hemispherical combustion chambers.

Ignition was by two magnetos, one for each bank of cylinders. With a compression ratio of 6.5:1, the motor put out 335 hp at 8600 rpm.

The radiator was mounted in front of the driver's foot pedals, while the engine was placed immediately behind the driver followed by the transaxle and the 200 liter fuel tank. The ladder style frame was a light and simple affair of tubular construction.

The independent suspension was a new innovation for the Portello works. The front suspension consisted of upper and lower 'A' arms acting on longitudinal torsion bars while the rear adopted a De Dion design with a Watts linkage, half shafts, and longitudinal torsion bars. Both the front and rear were damped by a combination of one telescopic

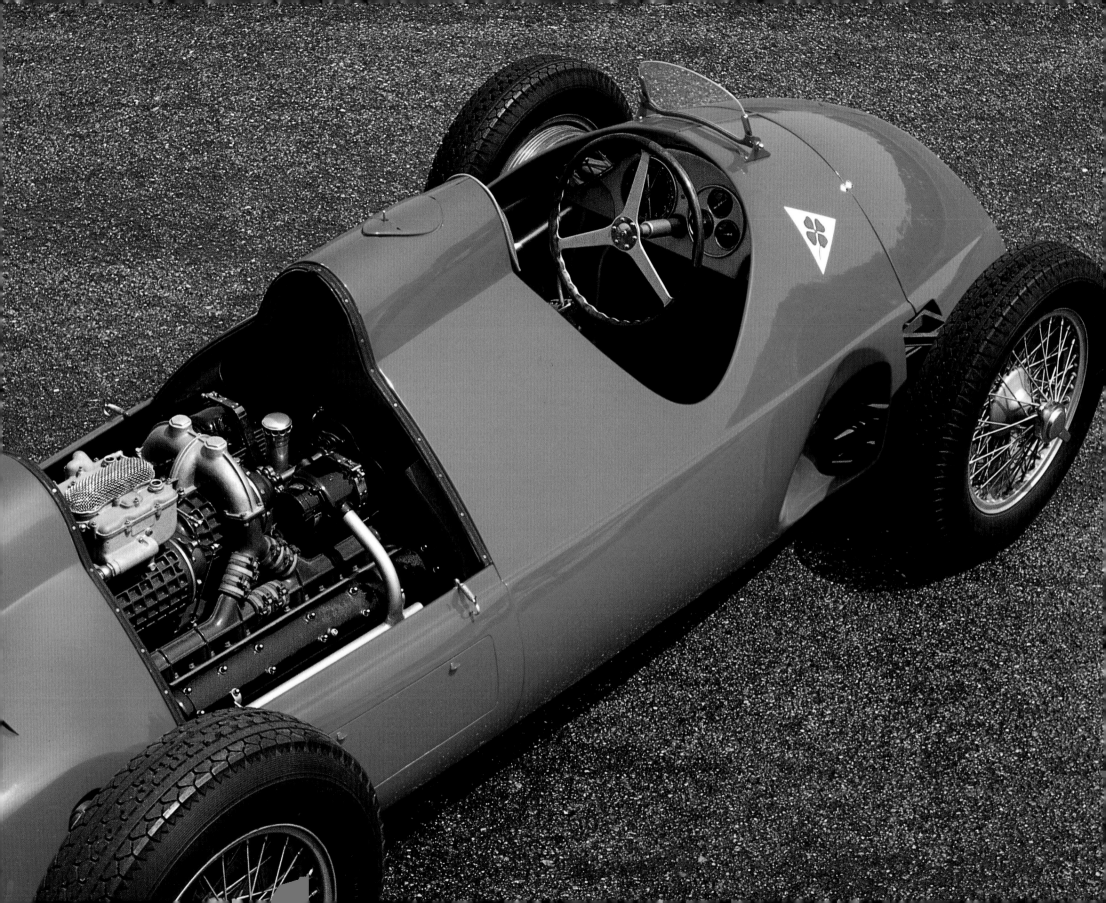

and one friction shock absorber per wheel

A further innovation on the 512 was the addition of a third brake shoe to the front drum brakes. The tires varied from the front to the rear, with the sizes being 5.25x17 and 7.00x18 respectively. With a dry weight of 710 kg, the Alfa 512 could reach a maximum of 300 kmph.

The name 512 came from a combination of the size of the engine, 1500 cc, and the 12 cylinders.

In 1940 and 1941 parts for three of these exotic racers were constructed, but only two prototypes were ever assembled. By 1943 the 512 had undergone several test sessions at the racetrack at Monza, but with the closing days of W.W.II, Alfa Romeo faced hard times and was forced to abandon testing the car.

The car pictured on these pages is preserved in its original state at the Alfa Romeo Museo Storico at Arese. With but a glance, one can see the exceptional level of design that Alfa Romeo achieved in the 1940s.

6C 2500 SS "1947": THE LAST OF A GENERATION

Italy's defeat in World War II left desolation of apocalyptic proportions. The huge factories of northern Italy, which had been dragged into the desperate war effort, were reduced to rubble by the air raids and invasions of various foreign armies. The Portello works, which in 20 years had become the most prestigious symbol of the national automobile industry, was almost completely destroyed. With the destruction of the factory and its tooling shops disappeared many relics of historical and racing significance to the Milanese manufacturer.

Nevertheless, the iron will to begin again from nothing showed that the workers' large sacrifices for Alfa were not totally lost. The factory was reconstructed for the better, with machinery acquired from war reparations. By May 1946, the factory was already up and running, building first of all metal furniture, aluminum framed windows, and gas ranges; by the end of that year cars were being built again, with a few of the 6C 2500 series being assembled from parts left over from the early war years.

In 1946 Alfa once again returned to the world of racing. It put the single-seat 158, a carryover from prewar days, on the race track at the first postwar Grand Prix. In June it raced at St. Cloud near Paris, in July at Geneva, and in September at Turin and Milan. These four races began with a defeat in France due to transmission problems; in the last three, glorious victories were achieved by Nino Farina,

Achille Varzi, and Carlo Felice Trossi. Such significant successes created an atmosphere of euphoria among the engineers at Portello, especially important given the difficult process of revitalizing the company during the rehabilitation of Italy.

During this exciting period, auto production could not achieve the company's ambitious goals. As a result Alfa Romeo concentrated on the 6C 2500 model. Technically, the car remained at the forefront of the auto industry, but for obvious reasons it did little to resolve the grave crisis of putting cars back on the roads of Italy. The new series of 1947 berlinas, with two new "Freccia d'oro" (golden arrow) coupés, had a vast potential on the profitable foreign markets. The success of this car proved the lasting value of Alfa Romeo, and renewed the huge prestige that it had achieved among racing aficionados around the world.

Apart from outward appearances, the 2500 model showed very few mechanical changes from the 1939 to the 1947 model. Improvements were made to the handling of the car and the pistons and the connecting rod bearings were refined to improve their wear.

The cylinder displacement remained the same at 2443 cc (72x100 mm), but the compression ratio was reduced to 7:1 on the 90 hp Sport version, and to 7.5:1 on the Super Sport, which produced 105 hp at 4800 rpm.

As far as the gearbox was concerned, the first and second gears were synchronized and the gearshift was moved to the column. In the rear of the car, the two pair of telescopic shocks were replaced with two larger diameter single shocks built by Alfa. The wire wheels featured aluminum rims with steel spokes and hubs, as did most racing wheels. They were shod with 6.50x17 tires as opposed to the 5.50x18 of the previous model.

The Super Sport chassis, with a wheelbase of 270 cm, was produced until 1951 for a total of 383 cars. Most of these went directly to Touring for the Superleggera coupé body, and the rest went to Pinin Farina for a cabriolet body. With a dry weight of 1400 kg, these custom-made cars could easily reach 165 kmph.

The two-seat cabriolet built by Pinin Farina during 1947 appears on these pages. Today this car kept in a private collection and is a splendid example of how the mechanics at Alfa put together the 2500 SS as a real work of art.

Renowned within Italy and abroad, the 2500 SS received many prestigious awards. At the various Concours d'Elegance of the time the Alfa 2500 SS always received awards or honorable mentions for its sleek lines and refined markings.

ALFETTA 159: THE VICTORIOUS SINGLE-SEATER

supercharged engine in anticipation of the new "Voiturette" racing class. By the beginning of 1938 four examples of the car were under construction at Modena. They were named "158", a contraction in honor of the 1500 cc engine and its 8 cylinders.

Alfa entered competition with the 195 hp prototypes. They placed first with Emilio Villoresi at the wheel, second with Clemente Biondetti, and seventh with Francesco Severi. A slender and elegant car, the exceptional agility that the 158 demonstrated at this race earned it the now famous nick-name, "Alfetta."

There were other successes in the 1938 racing season. In September at the Gran Prix Città di Milan, Villoresi and Severi raced to place first and second, but not without certain problems. In 1939, the 158 returned to win the Coppa Ciano with Farina driving, the Coppa Acerbo with Biondetti at the helm, and in the voiturette class at the Grand Prix of Switzerland with Farina behind the wheel. In 1940 at the Grand Prix of Tripoli, three of the 158s with 225 hp engines succeeded in clenching the top three places with Farina, Biondetti, and Trossi driving. One month

G ioachino Colombo, who had worked side by side with auto designer Vittorio Jano, was transferred in 1937 from the factory at Portello to Scuderia Ferrari. There he was assigned to lay out plans for a single-seated car with a 1500 cc

later, with Italy's entrance into the war, a halt was put to racing (for the moment) and the Alfettas was put aside and were evacuated from the factory so as not to be put at risk by aerial bombardment.

The 158 returned to the track in 1946 with Farina wining at Geneva with a specially tuned 254 hp version. This powerful car won again at Turin with Varzi driving and at Milan with Trossi. The next year the new Formula One class began and the Alfetta found success with Jean Pierre Wimille driving at Berne and at Spa, with Varzi racing at Bari, and with Trossi at Milan. In the racing year of 1948 Trossi triumphed at Berne, while Wimille won in France and twice in Italy, at the Grand Prix d'Italia in Turin and at the Grand Prix dell'Autodromo in Monza. By now, the engine's power had been increased to 310 hp.

After 13 consecutive victories, 1949 ended up being a year of relative inactivity. One of the highlights, however, was squeezing 350 hp at 8500 rpm out of the 158 engine. The Portello works, therefore, eagerly awaited the 1950 season. It was to be the most glori-

Nino Farina competing in the Grand Prix of Belgium at Spa in 1951.

ous year of victories in the long career of the Alfetta: in 11 races it achieved 11 victories. Juan Manuel Fangio won in Sanremo, Monaco, Belgium, France, Geneva, and at Pescara. Nino Farina won in Great Britain, Switzerland, Bari, and at Monza (where he was named World Champion). In this last race, Alfa Romeo entered two versions of the 159, a car which evolved from the 158.

This single-seater, which raced from victory to victory in spite of the competition and the passing years, had an in-line eight cylinder motor of 1479 cc (58x70 mm). The crankcase and separate cylinder assembly were cast in light alloy with the pistons running in steel liners. The crankshaft ran in nine babbit lined bronze bearings. The non-detachable cylinder heads incorporated

hemispherical combustion chambers, dual overhead cam shafts, and valves inclined at 100 degrees. The fuel was fed through a triple choke Weber downdraft carburetor into a low pressure Roots compressor followed by a high pressure Roots compressor. With its compression ratio of 6.5:1, the 159 motor produced 425 hp at 9300 rpm. The gearbox consisted of four speeds and reverse; while the body was fabricated of sheet metal wrapped around a multi-tube chassis. For rear suspension the 159 used a De Dion system with triangular structures on top connected to a transverse leaf spring; the front independent suspension consisted of trailing arms sprung also with a transverse leaf spring. The front tires measured 5.50x17, with the rears slightly larger at 7.00x18.

World Champion Juan Manuel Fangio in a 159 Alfetta in 1951.

1900: A TURNING POINT IN HISTORY AT PORTELLO

Three different prototypes of the 1900, each looking more like the one that entered into mass production. These photos were taken in 1950, slightly before the 1900 officially debuted.

On 4 May 1950, the first day of the 32nd Salone dell'Automobile at Turin, there were many disappointed spectators. During the prior week, it had been announced that the new two liter Alfa Romeo berlina would be presented, but Alfa delayed the debut. Instead, the new prototype was parked casually outside the Turin Exposition during the following week. Alfa seemed to be intent on impressing the public and playing with its curiosity, a test of the market's interest in their latest creation.

The 1900 was not an easy project to get underway. Alfa Romeo was going through difficult financial times in the years directly fol-lowing the war. In the workshops, one would find many of the tried and true technical strengths of Alfa, but a new industrial management style was being adopted that would permit the factory to build competitively priced cars that would appeal to a larger audience. The challenge, for the most part, was put on the shoulders of the engineer Orazio Satta, who had come to Portello in 1938 and in 1946, after the departure of Ricart, had assumed responsibility for Alfa's new designs.

Since the 1930s Alfa's seasoned staff of engineers and mechanics had expanded their skills through the creation of competition cars and aircraft engines, these skills were

now put to use in the creation of the 1900. The motor was a new in-line four cylinder of 1884 cc (82.55x88 mm) with cast iron block and aluminum head with hemispheric combustion chambers. The valves, inclined at 90 degree angles, were operated by chain driven dual overhead camshafts. Carburetion was by a single downdraft Solex. With a compression ratio of 7.5:1, the motor produced 90 hp at 5200 rpm, exceptional power for its time. The gearbox had four speeds and reverse, operated by a column mounted shift lever.

The chassis no longer used a separate frame, but rather adopted the modern solution of a unibody structure. The independent front suspension consisted of double 'A' arms and coil springs; in the rear a solid axle supported on large springs was anchored to the frame by two trailing arms and a Panhard rod (which was almost immediately substituted by a central triangle arm). Telescopic, hydraulic shocks were placed on all four wheels. The brakes relied on large diameter finned aluminum drums. The tires were either 6.00x16 or 165x400. With a dry weight of 1100 kg, the 1900 achieved a maximum speed of 150 kmph.

The new Alfa Romeo, originally produced at the rate of 15 a day, was a huge success among the upper middle class and the emerg-

ing middle class. The Italian government and many large corporations used the 1900 as their official car, not to mention sporting clients who liked the car for competitive road events. It clenched its first triumph at the Giro di Sicilia in 1951 and was featured in newspaper reports of autosports throughout the 1950s. It continually won in the categories of Turismo and International Turismo, from the Mille Miglia to the Coppa delle Dolomiti, from the Rallye Monte Carlo to the Carrera Panamericana. Because it achieved so many victories in Italy and other countries, it earned the nick-name "the family car that wins races."

From the basic model, the factory derived many different versions. Already by 1951 the T.I. version had appeared with a 100 hp engine. In 1954 the berlina Super was released with a 1975 cc engine and an unchanged output of 90 hp. In the same year, the T.I. Super appeared with two downdraft Solex carburetors and an output of 115 hp. During the period of 1951 to 1954, 8,183 units of the first berlina model were produced, while from the years 1954 through 1959, 9,060 Supers were built. Today, not many examples of the 1900 remain. Most of them, like the ones appearing on these pages, are in immaculate condition and are in the hands of collectors.

1900 C SPRINT CABRIOLET: THE THRILL OF THE CONVERTIBLE

Two photographs of the 1900 C Sprint Cabriolet taken in the courtyard of the factory at the beginning of the 1950s.

T he 1900 Berlina of 1950 was a realization of the esthetics of the moment, inspired by the new canon that was all the rage in the United States. This style featured clean surface development with the fenders flowing smoothly in one continuous line from the front to the tail. The body was rounded with slightly curved side panels, a curved windshield and rear window; and elongated hood and short trunk. The proto-

types of the new Alfas in the spring of 1950 were without a doubt curiosities. Except for the characteristics of the car's front end, which undoubtedly bore the Alfa touch, the personality of the car was far too similar to other mass-produced berlinas in Europe at the time. But it did sport its share of innovations, with the short, tapered tail giving this Portello creation a distinctly graceful look.

It was from this beginning that one of the smoothest berlinas was given life, a car that played an important role in the wide universe of European automobiles. Following Alfa Romeo's commercial success with the 2300

and the 2500, the 1900 was considered a special opportunity for Alfa to produce a car destined for foreign markets. To realize this dream, the 1900 L was built, with a touring sized motor and a berlina wheelbase of 263 cm. The Alfa 1900 C soon followed, fitted with a 100 hp T.I. motor and a wheelbase shortened to 250 cm.

The design of the coupé model was entrusted to Touring of Milan, a tribute to the two companies' collaboration for more than 20 years. The cabriolet was designed by Pininfarina of Turin, which had recently produced some splendid convertible bodies for the 6C 2500 SS.

524762 VI

It was from this high class carrozzeria that the inspiration to create the 1900 Sprint Cabriolet came. Entering production in 1951, the Cabriolet evolved through various series, with slight variations in the fenders, for a total of 88 cars built.

At the beginning of the 1950s, the three major Italian automobile manufacturers gave up on the idea of building cars with separate frames and instead adopted unibody construc-tion. As the bodies were now a structural part of the automobile, the coachbuilders were forced to find alternate ways of constructing special-ized bodies in order to compensate for the absence of a supporting frame. In developing a convertible body for the 1900, Pininfarina faced the long and arduous task of engineering a structurally sound floor-pan. Their design innovations gave the carrozzeria a decided edge for years to come.

The 1900 Sprint Cabriolet, which can be admired in the photographs on these pages, glows with the classic traits and esthetics that Pininfarina poured into other cars of the era. This Alfa Romeo achieved a sporting look in a formal and compact package which exhibited a distinctive classical balance. The 1900 incorporated the heart shaped center grille flanked by two side grilles that had become an Alfa trademark, regard-less of the carrozzeria responsible for the design.

1900 C SPRINT COUPÉ: TOWARDS NEW FRONTIERS

On top. A 1900 C Sprint Coupé of the first series, before the "Superleggera". Above. An example of the second series. The vertical chrome pieces on the bumper foreshadowed the Super Sprint version.

The Portello legacy had matured from the inspired technical design of the berlina models to commercial success with the granturismo coupés. Alfa now hoped to capture this same grand tradition with a 1900 Coupé. The elegance of the 6C 2500 SS, a coupé designed by Carrozzeria Touring, had become famous at Concours d'Elegance, and had paved the way for a new 2 liter version. Envisioned to satisfy the tastes of a less aristocratic clientele, this model appealed to a broad audience more likely to influence the future of Alfa Romeo. Touring was entrusted with the bodywork for the 1900 Sprint, with the ambition of interpreting to the letter the renovated tradition of the Italian touring car.

The design of the latest 1900 debuted in December 1950. Developed using "Superleggera" bodywork, it had a new stylistic approach, while incorporating from the berlina the three ovoid grills, one vertical in the middle and two lateral at the sides. It also borrowed some ideas from the elegant 2500 Villa d'Este of the previous year, most notably the lines of the roof and rear fenders. The 1900 differed from its forerunners with the enlarged windshield and small slightly curved trapezoidal rear window. The car is a two + two, with a light and cozy interior. It achieves a mastery of visual lightness in the lower body through the use of a scalloped section running along the lower edge of the doors.

The 1900 Sprint Coupé's mechanicals were derived from those of the berlina. It retained four cylinder, 1884 cc (84.5x88 mm) motor with double overhead cams. Thanks to the increase in compression ratio to 7.75:1, the enlargement of the valves, and a dual choke Weber carburetor, the engine output was increased to 100 hp at 5500 rpm. The

transmission remained essentially the same as the 1900 berlina, as well as the suspension, the steering wheel, and the brakes.

The body was made from sheets of aluminum formed by hand and clipped to a framework welded up from small tubes. In total, it weighed 100 kg less than the 1900 berlina, and didn't even pass the 1000 kg mark. With a slight increase in power and a considerable reduction of weight, the 1900 Sprint could cruise at 130 kmph, an incredible speed for the era and for a car with such a small engine.

About 800 of the 1900 Sprints were built at Carrozzeria Touring between 1951 and the first months of 1954, at which time the first series was replaced by the second. In June of the same year, this was replaced by the Super Sprint model, with a 1975 cc motor of 115 hp. This model was characterized by different front grilles and larger windows, a chrome strip highlighting the bottom of the doors, and more ample bumpers. The 1900 Sprint was much loved by its owners, especially those who used it for road racing. It was sold directly from the

Alfa car dealerships and was a runaway commercial success. During a time when the flux in demand for cars varied dramatically, the vigorous craftsmanship and high standards at Touring kept the 1900 C a sound buy.

When the Sprint went into production in 1951, three of the extra light cars were built with tubular bumpers, slight variations in the rear of the car, and with Plexiglas windows. One of these, which has been meticulously restored, can be appreciated in the photos on these pages.

GIULIETTA SPRINT: THE DREAM OF THE ITALIANS

Two photographs of the Giulietta Sprint prototype. The most noticeable difference between it and the Sprint that went into production is the side opening rear hatch and window.

The intense technical renovation at the beginning of the 1950s gave Alfa a new, more modern identity. After 25 years of making sixes and eights, Alfa abandoned the multi-cylinder engines and re-introduced the four cylinder, thereby opening up numerous commercial prospects. This boost was sorely needed considering Alfa's problems with management at the factory. In this atmosphere the type 750 was born, the project which led to the creation of the Alfa Romeo Giulietta. Forcefully pushed into production by the dynamic new director general at Portello, Francesco Quaroni, the Giulietta was devel-

oped by Orazio Satta and by a group of workers managed by Giuseppe Busso, who entrusted the technical aspects to Rudolf Hruska.

The architecture of this latest model came from a bold new concept: the extensive use of aluminum in the engine's block, cylinder head, front cover, and intake manifold, as well as the gearbox and differential casings all served to keep weight to a minimum. The motor displaced 1290 cc (74x75 mm) and featured silent chain-driven dual overhead camshafts and hemispherical combustion chambers with valves inclined at 80 degrees. The brilliant result was an engine so simple and robust that its variations would remain in production for more than 40 years.

The gearbox had four speeds and reverse operated by a column mounted shift lever. The car soon became famous for its extraordinary maneuverability. The independent front suspension copied the 1900's scheme of upper and lower 'A' arms with coil springs, an anti-sway bar, and telescopic shock absorbers. In the rear, the Giulietta again used the solid rear axle configuration of the 1900 with trailing arms plus a center

triangular link for location and telescopic shock absorbers for damping.

The brakes were another of the strong points of the Giulietta in the world of contemporary automobiles. They consisted of large diameter aluminum drums, the two front brakes with helical cooling fins and the rears with radial fins. The tires measured 155x380 on the 15 inch wheels.

Preparing the berlina's body for production caused long delays in its introduction. To make use of this time and to satisfy a clamoring public, the management at Alfa decided to market a limited series 2+2 coupé which would become the famous Giulietta Sprint. Its stylistic design, which had been roughed out by Portello in 1952 for use as a development mule, was turned over to Franco Scaglione of Bertone and Felice Mario Boano of Ghia for refinement. Finally, in the spring of 1954, Carrozzeria Bertone was entrusted with the Sprint's production. At Alfa, this new coupé came to be considered a blessing despite all the indecision and hesitation in making the berlina model. Initially the management at Alfa intended to market a small number of the

coupés, only a total of about 50. However, when they put the engineer, Rudolf Hruska, on the project, he convinced them that they had to make at least 1,000 Sprints.

On 21 April 1954, on the first day of the Salone dell'Automobile di Torino, the Giulietta Sprint made its official debut. The motor had a compression ratio of 8.5:1 and was fed via a Solex two-barrel downdraft carburetor. The engine could produce 65 hp at 6000 rpm, which was outstanding for the era. The new coupé had a length of 398 cm, a width of 152 cm, a height of 132 cm, and an empty weight of 890 kg. It could reach a top speed of 165 kmph.

The success of the Sprint, with simple but elegant bodywork by Bertone, was so quick that it upset plans at Alfa Romeo. Many clients could afford it, and they all wanted one. The Giulietta was immediately put in the spotlight, with its beautiful design and extraordinary handling. Quick, secure, with good braking and outstanding road manners, the Sprint was soon a protagonist in the world of road racing. Above all, the Sprint Veloce, Sprint Speciale and the Sprint Zagato dominated the racetrack for a decade in the 1300 Granturismo class. It also contributed to the economic recovery of Alfa, which produced 24,084 examples of the car between the years 1954 and 1962. One of these is pictured here, kept with loving care since it was built in the first months of 1955. It is a rare testament to the legendary and ageless style of Alfa Romeo.

GIULIETTA: ONE OF THE FAMILY

The front and the rear of a Giulietta taken in March 1955 for an Alfa brochure.

The design of the 1900 model underwent many revisions until 1952 when its final form was projected decisively into the Alfa Romeo Giulietta. The goal was a four-door small displacement berlina that was more ambitious than the models any

other company had created. The motor would have between 1100 and 1500 cc, a more utilitarian size than its predecessors. Alfa visualized a car that, compared with the multitude of 1100 cc cars of that time, could boast superior technical design with a price that would put it within the reach of the general public.

After the first days of research, Alfa opted for a motor of 1300 cc and for a compact body with a simple but luxurious interior. In the first place, the new car had to grasp the enthusiasm that the 1900 had received, which was already considered by many to be the most stable and brilliant berlina on the

market. The technical development of the car didn't bring any major difficulties, but much research was put into achieving the road handling for which Alfa was famous. In the second place the car needed to provide comfort in a berlina marketed to the middle class. It was imperative to have a silent,

smooth drive, which was a serious obstacle for the designers and test drivers of the first Giulietta prototypes.

In mid-1953, while the mechanical details of the car were already being considered, there remained unsolved problems with the unitized body, and Alfa had to delay the car's debut. Management had to rework the financing of the Giulietta project, admitting to the bankers at Finmeccanica that their ambitious debut for the Giulietta berlina would be late, that their sales projections were uncertain, and that the car was still in the design stage. To avoid the shame that was eating away at Portello and to avoid divisions within the IRI management at Alfa, it was decided to temporarily set aside the four-door model and to immediately produce a limited series of a coupé version, which appeared in 1954 as the Giulietta Sprint.

Presented one year later at the Salone di Torino, the Giulietta berlina carried forward the basic mechanical aspects of the coupé. The displacement of the motor was unchanged at 1290 cc (74x75 mm). With a compression ratio of 7.5:1 and single barrel Solex downdraft carburetor, it produced 50 hp at 5200 rpm, which was almost immediately increased to 53 hp at 5500 rpm and by 1961 reached 62 hp at 6000 rpm. From the Giulietta berlina was derived the T.I. version in 1957 with an output of 65 hp at 6100 rpm, which in 1961 was revised to achieve 74 hp at 6200 rpm.

Even though the lines of the Giulietta berlina weren't as fluid and esthetically pleasing as the Sprint, the berlina immediately attracted public acclaim. Its appearance, which was somewhat squarish and perhaps overly solid looking, was devoid of the refinements of the other Alfas. Even so, its lines were harmonious, and it had the extraordinary road handling that set Alfa apart from the crowd. With a dry weight of 915 kg and the capability to reach 140 kmph on the straight-away, it compared well with the 1500 cc five-seater berlinas of the time. The basic version stayed in production until 1966 and in this time there were 39,057 cars produced. Of the T.I. version, even more loved by the general public, there were 90,000 produced between 1957 and 1963. The Giulietta appearing on these pages, built in 1957 and preserved in excellent condition, represents an example of a car that may be simple in design but can claim an exalted lineage.

GIULIETTA SPIDER: THE INCREDIBLE HANDLING CONVERTIBLE

An early example of the Giulietta Spider photographed in 1955. The vertical chrome overriders on the bumper were slightly "baroque" in style and were later refined.

The excitement that greeted the Giulietta Sprint caused an important shift in the public's view of automobiles. Sporting a 1300 cc motor and an interior big enough for a medium sized family, this Alfa touring coupé provoked widespread interest in the possibility of a practical car that had all the mystique of an Alfa Romeo. The Sprint offered for the first time the opportunity to drive a car with a brilliant temperament that was secure and easy to control. Maybe most important, its price was comparable to other berlinas.

Riding this wave of popular euphoria, a second phase of Giuliettas appeared. Although the marketing was not closely orchestrated by Alfa Romeo, the second phase became at least as important as the first. The importer of Alfa in the United States, Hoffman Motor Car Company of New York, thought that a spider version of the new model Alfa would provide an excit-ing alternative to the unreliable British road-sters which were extremely popular among young automobile enthusiasts in America. Alfa Romeo approached the idea with some reluctance but built 600 cars for this single client. They asked both Bertone and Pininfarina to each produce two prototypes, allowing Alfa to see the possibilities of a spi-der for their overseas market. The race for a

contract was won by Pininfarina, whose elegant design was inspired by their work on the Lancia Aurelia B24, considered to be one of the most esthetically pleasing and sophisticated cars of the time.

Low and refined, with a rakish hood sloping forward to the heart shaped center grille and two side grilles now typical of Alfa, the Spider was based on the Sprint but with a wheelbase reduced to 220 cm. The motor displaced 1290 cc and produced 65 hp at 6500 rpm. With a dry weight of 860 kg, this model could easily reach speeds of 165 kmph. The interior held two seats, a dashboard with three large dials, and a long gear shift on the floor (the column shifter only appeared on the very first examples of the spider).

The beauty and the agility of its design, its focus on touring, and the decision to keep it a two-seater were all factors in making the Giulietta Spider a lightning success. It was very different from the contemporary English roadsters as this incredible convertible not only possessed great rigidity and handling dynamics but it included such amenities as roll-up windows and a watertight top.

With such a huge success in America, and despite the views of many pessimists, the new Spider soon made its debut in Italy and the other European markets. It was officially displayed at the Salon de Paris in 1955, and for the first time in Italy at the Salone di Torino in 1956, although deliveries didn't begin until almost a year later.

The Giulietta Spider gained fame outside of the specialized automobile crowd. It became the most refined car in stylish circles, longed for by the young of high society and by touring car aficionados. On tortuous race-tracks it kept up with, if not stayed ahead of, the granturismo cars of the time. The Spider owed its long career to its huge commercial success and many victories on the racetrack, mainly in the United States.

Soon, more powerful models were pro-duced. An 80 hp version appeared, then the Spider Veloce with a 90 hp engine. Of the original Spider model, 14,300 cars were built by 1962. One of these, which was built in 1956 and is still in perfect condition, appears on these pages. The Giulietta Spider.is like a fantasy that will never fade, as modern day collectors continue to search out this memen-to from the roaring 1950s.

GIULIETTA SZ: THE RETURN OF ALUMINUM

These are two examples of solutions that Zagato tried for the Giulietta SZ "round tail" of the time: with the front lights covered in Plexiglas (above), and without the covers (below). The streamlining covers helped the car's aerodynamic lines, but was not always appreciated by its buyers.

Du) uring the touring season of 1955 and the beginning of 1956, the Giulietta Sprint was the most raced car on the road. But already by the spring of 1956, with the debut of the 90 hp Sprint Veloce, a challenger had entered the arena. The Giulietta SV became the most sought after Alfa coupé of the day, with aspirations to great success. The challenge was soon resolved at the 23rd Mille Miglia, when a Sprint Veloce took the trophy in the 1300 cc Granturismo class, placing eleventh over all.

The drivers and the race crews, however, had higher goals. In the summer of that year, the Giulietta SV won at the 100 kilometers of Nürburgring, at the Coppa delle Dolomiti, at the Aosta-Gran San Bernardo, and in many other competitions on the race track and on road circuits. In spite of these victories, the weight of the car was considered too excessive to take advantage of the great mechanical aspects of the car. Carrozzeria Zagato, which had specialized since the 1920s and 1930s in creating aluminum bodies (they had done so for the invincible Alfa 6C and Alfa 8C) put its experience to the test by dismantling a crashed Sprint Veloce and designing a body with a sleeker profile which weighed much less than the original. This prototype was built more for competition by a private cus-

tomer than as a proposal to Alfa for a new production model Giulietta. At the wheel of the aluminum bodied SV was Massimo Leto of Priolo. His was a huge success at the Intereuropa Cup on September 2, 1956 at the racetrack at Monza.

This fortunate debut marked the beginning of a long season of successes for this new version of the Giulietta. From 1957 to 1959, Zagato produced SVZs to special order using the chassis of customer supplied Sprint Veloces, which had a wheelbase of 238 cm.

Beginning in 1960, Alfa began supplying Zagato with the floorpan and running gear designed for the Giulietta Sprint Speciale which had a reduced wheelbase of 225 cm. The technicians at Alfa Romeo worked long and hard to re-engineer the 1290 cc engine. The changes included a 9.7:1 compression ratio, two twin choke side-draft Weber carburetors, high lift/long duration cam shafts, forged pistons, a large capacity finned aluminum sump, and free flow tubular exhaust headers. Output increased to a reliable 100 hp at 6500 rpm. In addition, a five-speed gearbox from the 2000 was used, and the front brakes were changed to a high efficiency, three leading shoe design acting on steel lined aluminum drums, while the radially finned rear drums were replaced by the larger diameter helical drums as used in the front.

Zagato designed a very compact body, with fenders drawn tautly around the wheels, which was a delicate feat for a car that would race on mountain roads. The streamlining of the front lights, the oval-shaped rear, and the extremely low front revealed the results of accurate aerodynamic research, conducted not in a wind tunnel, but rather during extensive road testing. The result was a round, short coupé with a smooth body and an empty weight of 785 kg. Most importantly, the Giulietta SZ broke the barrier of 200 kmph.

It debuted May 15, 1960, at the Gran Premio di Napoli, where Sergio Pedretti triumphed in the 1300 cc Granturismo class. He then continued for the rest of that season and into 1961 to collect victory after victory, always with enhanced mechanical parts by such pros as Virgilio Conrero and Piero Facetti. Between 1961 and 1962, 213 examples of the Giulietta Sprint Zagato were produced and sold. These went, for the most part, to racing teams and private race car drivers around the world.

One of the surviving cars, pictured on these pages, is preserved by a Tuscan collector. (The wheels aren't stock, although they were used at the time to further reduce the car's weight.) This particular car had a great racing career and was passed from Alfa Romeo to the Scuderia S. Ambroeus in the 1970s and later to the Scuderia Centro Sud. In 1961, this rare Giulietta SZ, a 1300 cc berlinetta, was timed on the Autostrada del Sole, at a speed of 213 kmph, an incredible speed even for today.

2000 SPRINT: GRANTURISMO ACCORDING TO BERTONE

The 2000 Sprint represents the work of Giorgetto Giugiaro, a young designer at Bertone. With this one Alfa Romeo he challenged the traditional canon of car design. The most noticeable change of his stylistic approach was the integration of the front lights into the grille.

A new reality had taken hold of the postwar Alfa Romeo. Beginning with the Alfa 1900, which was of unitized construction and built on an assembly line, the factory at Portello had been able to dramatically increase its productivity. In the second half of the 1950s, the incredible

performance of the car proved its worth as a technical success; its comfort and handling, however, couldn't insure that it would continue to sell. Work on a new project, the "2000," was begun.

In designing the 2000, Alfa used a four cylinder engine with 1975 cc (84.5x88 mm) and increased the compression ratio to 8.25:1. A twin choke down draft Solex carburetor was chosen, which helped raise the power from 90 hp to 105 hp. A five speed version of the Giulietta transmission was used in conjunction with a column shift. There were minor modifications to the steering wheel and to the braking system.

The 2000 debuted at the Salone di Torino in 1957 where it appeared as a beautiful, comfortable berlina, perhaps a little opulent with its complex design and flashy chrome. The wheelbase was 272 cm, with the track between the wheels being 140 cm in the front and 137 cm in the rear. The total length of the car was 471 cm and the width was 170 cm. With an empty weight of 1340 kg, the Alfa Romeo 2000 gave up a little of the incredible acceleration and agility of the 1900, but gained the status of being a much more noble car, an automobile with international class.

To "Alfisti" who craved more power, the technicians at Portello offered a Sprint version, a car that once again showed the spunk of the earlier Alfas. The new Sprint was a stylized, modern four-seat grand touring car. Its motor produced 115 hp at 5900 rpm, thanks to raising the compression ratio to 8.5:1 and using two dual choke Solex side-draft carburetors. The gearshift was moved from the column to the floor and the wheelbase was generously shrunk to 258 cm.

It was with the 2000 Sprint that Giorgetto Giugiaro of Bertone gave life to one of the most elegant and innovative auto bodies of the era. From the basic configuration of the Giulietta Sprint, he introduced original solutions to the 2000 Sprint's design. Drastically changing the styling of the nose of the car, he incorporated the front lights into the grille for the first time, which resulted in a more continuous line for the hood and the front fenders. This avant-garde approach had widespread impact on many other carrozzerias and became a standard on almost all cars to this day. The large front flowed harmoniously into the greenhouse of the car, with its ample windows, and then into the rear of the car, dominated by the large rear window and the rear lights insert into the rear panel.

These new classes of emerging automobiles were part of the magic of the "Italian Economic Miracle." The 2000 Sprint appeared in the autumn of 1960 as the symbol of this miracle in the automobile world. Its refined elegance and its four-seat comfort put this car at the summit of the most admired cars of its time. With a dry weight of 1200 kg, a length of 450 cm, and a width of 170 cm, the 2000 Sprint revealed itself to be an incredible-handling road car, capable of a maximum speed of 175 kmph. Only 700 of the 2000 series were produced before 1962, when it was redesigned with a six-cylinder engine and became known as the 2600 Sprint. Today, the 2000 Sprint—of which a splendid example appears on these pages—doesn't show its age of 35 years; instead it proves that it is still an aristocratic and fascinating automobile.

2600 SPIDER: THE REBIRTH OF SIX CYLINDERS

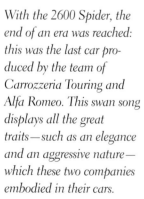

With the 2600 Spider, the end of an era was reached: this was the last car produced by the team of Carrozzeria Touring and Alfa Romeo. This swan song displays all the great traits—such as an elegance and an aggressive nature— which these two companies embodied in their cars.

oward the end of the 1950s, Alfa Romeo began to change. No longer the advanced laboratory specializing in high performance cars, the company had assumed the identity of a large industrial plant, assembling full series of new cars

rather than limited editions. In 1959 production reached 23,184 units, almost double the number of cars that had been produced in Portello's first 40 years.

The Giulietta models had been well received, and the incredible success of the 1900 models for almost a decade consolidated Alfa's position in the market. With this stability, Alfa could afford to allow the engineer Satta and his group of technicians the liberty to test six-cylinder engines. The prestige of Alfa Romeo and its renown in producing high powered racers let it easily take advantage of the high end of the market, those who were interested in cars with more than four cylinders.

In designing the new motor, Alfa revived the blueprints of its four-cylinder dual overhead camshaft engine. The large engine of 2584 cc (83x79.6 mm) seemed to be a nostalgic return to the prewar 6C 2500, but the new 2600 held many surprises. The engine was cast in aluminum with replaceable wet steel cylinder liners. The valve gear followed Alfa's tradition of double overhead cams with silent chain drive operating valves inclined at 90 degrees which fed mixture to hemispheric combustion chambers.

From the beginning of the project, two models of the car were envisioned. The first was to be a berlina with two downdraft twin

choke Solex carburetors and a compression ratio of 8.5:1 producing 130 hp at 5900 rpm. Second, were the two more powerful versions, the Sprint and the Spider, with three twin choke side draft Solex carburetors, hotter camshafts, and a compression ratio of 9:1 producing 145 hp. The other systems in the car replicated those of the Alfa 2000, except for the brakes, which were changed from drums to disc brakes in the front. Beginning in 1963 all four wheels were converted to disc brakes.

The 2600 debuted at the Salon de Geneva in 1962 with three different bodies. These were slightly updated versions of designs used for a few years on the 2000 model. The Spider underwent a few touch ups on the front, the hood, and on the base of the sides. Produced by Carrozzeria Touring, the coachbuilder which had achieved its greatest splendor at the side of Alfa Romeo in the 1930s, the new Spider certainly captured the élan of the original Touring-bodied 2000 from 1957.

The specifications for the Spider were complex, and Touring was considered best suited to the task. Inspired by Pininfarina's success with the Giulietta Spider, the 2600 would have two short and compact seats. It needed an easy yet energetic feel to follow in the Giulietta Spider's footsteps, since that car had already been decreed an unsurpassed triumph.

The wheelbase was a short 250 cm, and though the 2600 Spider was a little boxy and impersonal, it did not lack detailed elegance. The lines resembled those of its contemporary, the Lancia Flaminia convertible, with which it was often in competition. Furthermore, the passenger compartment of the 2600 was sufficiently spacious to allow the two seats to be fully adjustable, making the car more appealing to clients who weren't content with simple bucket seats.

Although the coachbuilder's badge read Touring Superleggera, the 2600 Spider was of conventional steel construction with an empty weight of 1220 kg. The Spider, like the mechanically identical 2600 Sprint, was capable of a top speed of over 200 kmph.

This automobile was conceived for a wealthy clientele with an interest in touring cars. 2253 of the 2600 Spider were produced between 1962 and 1965. The car appearing on these pages is impeccably preserved in its original condition. It reawakens the nostalgia for a car which passed from the factory at Portello like a meteor: too fast and short lived.

GIULIA TZ: THE WEIGHT BATTLE IS WON

*Two photos of the
Giulia TZ's frame.
Achieving the least amount
of weight was the focus
of the designers
during its construction,
giving life to a car which
turned out to be extremely
competitive for many years.*

At the dawn of the 1960s, the Giulietta SZ was invincible on the racetrack. Driven by many private racers, the car gallantly kept alive the Alfa spirit at a time when Alfa Romeo wasn't focusing on its racing cars. But the SZ, although a great car, was

a compromise based on the Sprint Speciale coupé, designed for a clientele interested in a touring car that was not exclusively a racer.

At the Portello works, a time table was created for the design and production of a new racing berlinetta with even more sophisticated technology. The process, however, was moving slowly. Much of the emphasis in the factory at the time was on the production of large numbers of series produced cars such as the Giulia T.I. berlina, as opposed to specialized cars. The Giulia T.I., with its high specifications and exceptional mechanical reliability, would form the basis for this new berlinetta.

The first of the 105 series Giulias, this most famous of mid 1960s Alfa Romeos featured a 1570 cc (78x82 mm) version of the Giulietta dual overhead cam engine which developed 92 hp at 6200 rpm. The five speed transmission of the Giulietta Sprint Speciale was made standard while the front and rear suspensions were improved versions of those used on the 101 series Giuliettas.

In October 1962, after a grueling series of tests, the Giulia TZ debuted at the Salone di Torino. It was a competition car, with newly designed aluminum bodywork by Zagato wrapped around a framework of small diameter steel tubing. The light weight tubular frame

(from which the "T" in TZ came) weighed a mere 62 kg and the entire car just 660 kg. The long, sloping front fenders and hood were incorporated into a single piece which hinged forward for engine access. The body, which was designed with aerodynamics foremost in mind, was fitted tautly over the tubular framework and ended in a long and pronounced "Kamm" tail. It featured a very refined, though light weight, interior. With a wheelbase of 220 cm and a track of 130 cm, the TZ measured less than 395 cm in length, 151 cm in width and a very low 120 cm in height.

The motor was the now classic "Giulia" engine in Sprint Speciale tune, inclined at 20 degrees and moved back in the chassis for better weight distribution. With a compression ratio of 9.7:1 and two side draft Weber 40 DCOE carburetors, the engine was capable of producing 112 hp at 6500 rpm. The fifth gear ratio was changed from 0.79 to 0.85 and a limited slip differential was installed along with a new independent rear suspension design wherein the upper arm consisted of the axle half shaft while the lower arm was formed by a triangular strut with an enlarged base. Suspension was by a vertical strut which combined a coil spring with the telescopic shock absorber. Braking was via four-wheel discs, with the rears mounted inboard next to the differential for decreased unsprung weight. With its wind cheating body, light weight, and great power, this beautiful example of design and engineering could reach the incredible speed of 215 kmph.

The production of the Giulia TZ was entrusted to Delta, a company which had been founded the preceding year in the town of Udine by Ludovico Chizzola and Carlo Chiti. Production was begun in 1963, and between the years 1964 and 1967, 101 Giulia TZs were produced.

The new berlina first hit the racetrack at the Autodromo di Monza in November 1963 at the Coppa Fisa race, where driver Lorenzo Bandini claimed first place. Throughout the following years the TZ dominated the class of 1600 cc Gran Turismo racing cars. Beginning with the 12 Hours at Sebring in March 1964 followed by the Targa Florio, the 1000 km of Nürburgring, the 24 Hours of Le Mans, then the Tour de France, the Coupé des Alpes, the Tour de Corse, and the Criterium des Chevennes, the Giulia TZ raced to victory. The TZ was truly a great car, with an engine capable of producing as much as 170 hp at 7500 rpm in race tune. Some of these victories were again repeated in the 1965 racing season, and again on many racetracks and touring competitions between 1966 and 1968.

By developing a car built for speed, Alfa Romeo claimed its place once again as a producer of the finest racing automobiles. While many of the Giulia TZs disappeared in the following years, the rare surviving one appearing on these pages is in the attentive hands of an Alfa collector who has kept the car in its impeccable original condition.

GIULIA TZ 2: TOP COMPETITION

Alfa's victorious "Tubolares" were facing more and more competition on the racetracks. With other manufacturers producing cars to meet the challenge posed by Alfa Romeo, the Portello factory felt compelled to intensify their research, testing, and production of the next generation of racers. Delta, the workshop formed the preceding year by Carlo Chiti, transferred from the town of Udine to Milan under the new name, Autodelta. Their first project was the Giulia TZ, produced by special order according to the individual wishes of private racers.

In the course of 1964 the Giulia TZ 2 was born. A natural evolution from the tubular framed TZ, the TZ 2 was full of technical and esthetic innovations, creating a car with a unique personality.

The new Zagato berlinetta debuted at the Salone di Torino in October of that year, showcasing the extensive redesign of the car's mechanics and body. To reduce the height and improve the aerodynamics of the car for better handling, Autodelta modified the tubular frame to set the motor in a lower position. The driver's seat was modified into a reclining, elongated form. By abandoning the 15-inch wheels of the TZ model, and opting instead for 13-inch wheels, the car was further lowered to a height of only 102 cm, for

which Zagato created a compact body only 368 cm long. The Giulia TZ 2 hugged the road, a flattened lozenge of power fully 18 cm lower than its sister, the Giulia TZ.

The four-cylinder, dual overhead cam engine of 1570 cc was reworked, and by applying the latest innovations, horsepower was increased by 50 percent over that of the TZ. The pistons were lightened and slightly retooled, giving a compression ratio of 11.6:1, while a new cylinder head was adopted incorporating larger valves and two spark plugs per cylinder. The connecting rods, camshafts, and exhaust system were new, and the engine now featured dry sump lubrication. With these various modifications, the TZ 2 engine produced 165 hp at 7000 rpm in standard tune. The transmission remained the same as the Giulia TZ, while the different sized wheels required tires of 5.50x13 on the front and 6.00x13 on the rear.

Zagato continued to find ways to cut corners in weight. Applying the latest technology, they substituted fiberglass for the aluminum body, to create a total weight of a mere 620 kg. The Giulia TZ 2 was capable

of reaching a maximum velocity of 245 kmph.

In 1965, the same year it debuted on the racetrack, only 12 of the cars were produced. It ran well at the 1000 km di Monza, the 6 Hours at Melbourne, the 1000 km of Nürburgring, the Rallye Jolly Hotels, and at the Trento-Bondone race. In 1966, the successes at the 1000 km di Monza and Nürburgring were repeated, with victories also being claimed at the 12 Hours of Sebring, the Targo Florio, and at the Circuito del Mugello.

The splendid example illustrated on these pages is now in a private collection. Released by Autodelta in February 1966 it ran in the Targo Florio of that same year (placing fourth) and at the Rallye Jolly Hotels, not to mention the Trento-Bordone (first place in its class), at the Circuito del Mugello (first place in its class), at the Bolzano-Mendola race, and at the Coppa del Chianti Classico (first place overall). It was a car with a brilliant career and a very high level of competitive excellence which was withdrawn too early from the world of racing.

GIULIA SUPER: TYPICAL ITALIAN BERLINA

At the end of June 1962 Alfa Romeo presented the Giulia T.I. The crowds at the Autodromo di Monza were baffled by the nonconformist styling of the latest berlina. At the Portello works, the technicians had conceived a new car that was mechanically evolved from the Giulietta, but at the same time a step beyond the latest Giulietta.

The dramatic break from design stereotypes was, without a doubt, courageous. The curves of the Giulietta of the 1950s were replaced with solid square lines which, while not entirely original, were definitely striking in their boldness. The four front headlights were inspired by the 2000 Sprint. Both the widened fenders and the abruptly terminated lines of the "Kamm" tail contributed to a significant break with the styles of the moment, and reflected a new, highly functional esthetic.

Knowing that its radical look would create turmoil, Alfa billed the Giulia T.I. as the "automobile designed by the wind." Because its proven aerodynamic qualities were not evident to the untrained eye, many saw this as an

attempt to validate a rash stylistic move on the part of Alfa.

The new berlina had a wheelbase of 251 cm, with a front track of 132 cm, and a rear track of 127 cm. Most of the technical aspects of the new berlina were derived from the Giulietta, including the motor and transmission, but the front and rear suspension and the steering column were altered. There was a desire to downplay the new car's similarities with the Giulietta, and lowering the rear of the car as much as possible was an effective solution. But the changes in the design, combined with an improved gearbox, also enhanced the handling and control of the car. The double overhead camshaft four cylinder engine of 1570 cc (78x82 mm) which produced 92 hp at 6200 rpm, had the

same layout as the one first seen in the Giulietta in 1954.

The Giulia T.I. took the market by surprise, converting even its staunchest critics into enthusiastic supporters. The Portello works produced 7,026 examples in the second half of 1962, followed by 27,802 of the various versions in 1963. 21,560 Giulia T.I.s were produced in 1964, and 9,304 before March, 1965, when the Giulia Super debuted at the Geneva Auto Show.

The Super, one of the first true "sports sedans," represented an important stage in the evolution of the model. Its motor kept to the original design, but with an increase in the compression ratio from 8.5:1 to 9:1 and the adoption of a pair of 40 DCOE Weber carburetors as fitted to the Veloce models, the output reached 98 hp at 5500 rpm. The five-speed gearshift was moved to the floor next to the driver's seat, while the brakes were now discs on

all four wheels incorporating vacuum assist and dual circuitry for safety purposes.

Among the improvements to the body was a new, more luxurious interior with an improved dashboard and instrumentation. With a length of 415 cm, a width of 156 cm, and a height of 143 cm, the Giulia Super weighed 1040 kg. It could reach a maximum speed of 175 kmph, an unusually high speed for a series produced car of its class. Due to its exceptional performance, modern styling, advanced engineering, and excellent design, the Giulia Super enjoyed a long career, with a total of 126,000 cars sold by 1972. The example that appears on these pages was built in 1965, and remains one of the original Giulias that has survived to this day. It has been handed down to us intact, and represents the spirit of the entire generation of the Giulia, the best of the vintage Alfa Romeos.

GIULIA GTA: ALFA'S QUADRIFOGLIO CONTINUES TO RISE TO THE TOP

T he Giulia Sprint GT was shown for the first time at the Frankfurt Auto Show in September 1963. Alfa Romeo had Carrozzeria Bertone design the Sprint GT as a replacement for the 10-year-old Giulietta Sprint. This new model Giulia maintained the extremely high level of handling and driveability for which Alfa's sports cars were famous, and remained in Alfa's line-up, in all the different versions, for a good 14 years, reaching a total production of 192,000 units.

One year later, on top of the pomp and circumstance of the new Sprint GT, the GTA,

which was aimed toward buyers interested in racing, was officially introduced at the Amsterdam Auto Show in February, 1965.

Externally, the GTA (the "A" standing for Alleggerita, meaning lightened) remained unchanged with respect to the basic coupé body, except for the elimination of the chrome hubcaps on the wheels, the introduction of two little air intakes above the front bumper, and a thin chrome stripe along the front grille. The most distinguishing mark was the white triangle with the green quadrifoglio (four leaf clover) emblem placed on both front fenders and next to the rear license plate. The quadrifoglio was the traditional Alfa Romeo racing symbol dating from the 1924 success of the RL and symbolized the luck bestowed upon this new model of Alfa Romeo. The lightening of the body was accomplished by using aluminum panels for much of the bodywork, the elimination of all the soundproofing and the reduction of interior fittings. The dry weight of the vehicle was trimmed down to 745 kg, a net reduction of 200 kg from the normal GT version.

The motor of this latest Alfa, the twin cam 1570 cc (78x72 mm), underwent extensive modifications. Apart from the compression increase from 9:1 to 9.7:1, the diameter of the intake valves was increased from 35 to 40.5 mm, while the diameter of the exhaust valves—now filled with sodium for better cooling—increased from 31 mm to 36.5 mm.

The inclination of valves was also changed from 90 to 80 degrees. Due to there no longer being room between the larger valves for a centrally located spark plug, the head was modified to accept dual plugs. Two side draft Weber 45 DCOE carburetors took care of the gas flow. Thanks to these modifications the power in standard form increased to 115 hp at 6000 rpm. The brakes and the suspension remained unchanged while the five-speed transmission was fitted with close ratio gearing.

With more power and less weight the standard Giulia GTA could pass the 185 kmph mark, while the race-prepared version by Autodelta for the Alfa Romeo racing team was capable of reaching 220 kmph. The race-tuned version's motor, running a compression ratio of 10.5:1 and featuring improve-

ments to intake and exhaust flow developed 170 hp at 7500 rpm. Moreover, on these special cars an oil cooler was added, along with a limited-slip rear differential, more rigid suspension and 5.5x14 tires. The entire weight of the car was further reduced to 700 kg.

The Giulia GTA's racing debut was on March 20, 1966 at Monza with the team of De Adamich/Zeccoli taking victory in the Four Hours of the Jolly Club race. That year the GTA won just about everything, from the 4 Hours of Sebring to the 6 Hours of Nürburgring to the Race of Mugello. Then it blasted through Germany, Great Britain, Holland, Hungary, Belgium, and France, to win the first prize of the Coupé des Alpes. This sequence of successes for the unmatched Giulia GTA was topped by the conquest of the 1966 European Challenge for Touring Class cars. It won again in 1967 (when it asserted its authority in the European Championship for the touring class) and in 1968 on top of many other national championship awards.

As one of the key players in the history of modern sports car racing, 493 specimens of the GTA were produced up through 1969. Some of these still survive—like those whose photos accompany this text—perfectly restored and always objects of admiration and desire for the numerous lovers of racing Alfa Romeos.

SPIDER 1600 "DUETTO": CONTROVERSY AND FASCINATION

The idea to allow consumers to decide the name of the new spider, and all the publicity that this created for the marque of the serpent, launched the car's successful career. The above pictures show Alfa Romeo president,

Giuseppe Luraghi, as he is giving a Duetto as a prize to the man who submitted the winning name. This remained the official name of the model that continued to be commercially billed as the 1600 Spider.

A decade is a very long life for a sports car; to the fickle public, most models lose their polish in half this span. Somehow the Giulietta Spider cheated this rule. Introduced in 1955 for a younger clientele especially interested in speed, the

Spider had a clamorous success, much of it unexpected. It was as prized as the exceptional Sprint coupé, another Alfa that made the production roster for over a decade.

Twenty-five thousand of this compact, attractive car were built, with both 1300 cc and 1600 cc engines. The future of the design, however, was in serious doubt when the Portello works and the designers at Pininfarina began timidly to consider a substitute model in 1961. At the Salon de Geneva of that year, a prototype appeared of the Giulietta Spider Speciale Aerodinamica, designed by the famous Turin-based Carrozzeria Pininfarina. Many of the stylistic innovations of this car would reappear on future models. The latest version finally hit the market in 1966, once again in time to be shown at the Swiss autoshow.

The new car, with its 1600 motor, had a much more sophisticated design compared to the preceding Spider. But its updated body design wasn't spontaneously accepted; while much of the reaction was favorable, much of it was tepid as well. Perhaps there was already a nostalgia for the Giulietta of ten years earlier.

Alfa Romeo was unsure of what type of logo and what name to give the new model. Instead of naming the car in the executive boardroom, the public was invited to make the choice. Among the 140,000 responses, "Duetto" was the name that the judges thought best described the spirit of this two-seat speedster; the name also pays respect to the high quality engineering of the Alfa Romeo and Pininfarina duet. For many this seemed a cold name, too logical, with no emotional pull. At the Portello works, the car was baptized with the nickname "Osso di seppia," or "cuttle bone," because of the flat, almost symmetrical shape of the hood and tail whereas in the United States it was referred to simply as a round tailed spider.

The inner workings of the 1600 Spider "Duetto" sported a number of improvements compared to the Giulia 1600 Spider which had been in production since 1962. The original motor was the same dual overhead cam 1570 cc unit with a compression ratio of 9:1; the enlargement of the valves from 35 to 37 mm and the addition of two sidedraft 40 DCOE Weber carburetors, increased power

from 92 hp at 6200 rpm to 109 hp at 6000 rpm. The transmission in the Duetto was the same as in the Giulia GT, as was the suspension and the four wheel disc brakes.

The 1600 Spider Duetto, with its bodywork truly rich in original ideas, was the last car designed by Battista Pinin Farina before he died in April of 1966. The stretched out sloping nose with its Plexiglas headlight covers mirrored the racing cars of the day. Its scalloped sides and rounded tail were both elements that made the car stand out from its competitors.

The Duetto was put on a wheelbase of 225 cm, 10 cm less than the coupé version. The front track measured 131 cm and the rear 127 cm. The car was 425 cm long (85 cm longer than the Giulietta Spider), 163 cm wide (an increase of 9 cm), and weighed 990 kg. With the top down, it could reach a maximum speed of 185 kmph and could go 400 meters in 18 seconds from a stop.

Production of the first series of 1600 Spider Duettos in the two year period of 1966 and 1967 totaled 6,315. One of these, perfectly conserved in its original condition, is pictured on these pages. This fascinating Alfa Romeo was the object of much controversy but was nevertheless a champion in the continuing history of Alfa Romeo.

33 STRADALE: ON THE WINGS OF VICTORY

The 33 Stradale in two photos of the era: "closed" and "open." The car was designed for the racetrack and was then transformed, at least in appearance, for the domestic and commercial market. The 33 Stradale was the epitome of the supercar of the 1970s.

The official return of Alfa Romeo to the racetracks was marked in 1964. When the "33/2 liter" car hit the track in September of that year, it became apparent that Alfa would be playing to win. Designed for the "Gruppo Sport Prototipi" (Sport Class Prototypes), it revolutionized the philosophy of Alfa with its center mounted V8, bringing the marque in line with the competitive racing car makers.

The design of the 33 (then known as the 105.33) was put together by technicians under the management of the engineers Satta and Busso. The criteria were entirely

new, with a frame inspired by aeronautic technical design, consisting of three aluminum tubes of 200 mm in diameter layered in an asymmetric H shape. Within this H was placed the fuel tank, and at the extremes were fixed two structures of light alloy to which were attached the suspension, steering, motor, and the oil and water radiators.

The motor was a 90 degree V8 of 1995 cc (78x50.4 mm) with the block and heads cast of light aluminum alloy. There were two valves per cylinder, inclined at 48 degrees, and driven by two overhead cams per bank. With dry sump lubrication, a compression ratio of 11:1, and a Lucas fuel injection sys-

tem, the motor produced 260 hp at 9200 rpm.

The gearbox held six gears plus reverse. The front and rear suspension had transverse arms with coil over shock units and stabilizer bars. The dual circuit brakes consisted of outboard mounted front discs, with the rear discs mounted inboard next to the differential.

Alfa Romeo turned the development of the project over to Autodelta, where the engineer Carlo Chiti and his technicians spent much time testing and adjusting the prototype. The car was given an extremely light and open three-part fiberglass body. The 33/2 Sport Prototype weighed 670 kg and could reach a maximum of 275 kmph. After numerous test runs conducted

on the racetrack at Balocco in 1966, the car made its victorious debut in the cross-country race at Fléron, Belgium on March 13, of the following year. The car also had numerous successes during the years 1967 and 1968 in the 24 Hours at Daytona, the 24 Hours of Le Mans, and at Vallelunga, Mugello, Imola. The list goes on.

From these mechanical designs, the 33 Stradale was developed in 1967. It was a berlinetta marvelously crafted by Franco Scaglione and assembled in light alloy by the Carrozzeria Marazzi, which had built a solid reputation through its collaborations with Touring and Zagato. The resulting car had soft and harmonious lines, with a cut off "Kamm" tail, an enormous panoramic windshield, and long doors which opened upward towards the front. On the racing version, the wheelbase was lengthened to 235 cm (a 10 cm increase) with the central part of the frame being constructed of sturdy sheet steel.

The motor, which featured a double ignition system, Spica fuel injection, and a compression ratio of 10:1, produced 230 hp at 8800 rpm. The length of the car was 397 cm, the width was 171 cm, and the height was 99 cm. The dry weight was 700 kg with tires measuring 5.25x13 and 6.00x13. The 33 Stradale could reach 260 kmph, an extraordinary speed for a 2 liter car, especially considering that it was just a prototype.

Of the 50 cars expected to be produced, only 18 left the shop at Autodelta. One of these extremely rare cars appears on these pages in perfect condition.

MONTREAL: A GRAND PROJECT FOR THE EXPO

On top, one of the prototypes which appeared at the Montreal Expo in 1967.
Above, the definitive sketch by Bertone with modifications necessary to adapt the car to the powerful V8 engine from the Alfa 33.

For Montreal's Expo '67, Alfa Romeo was chosen to interpret the theme of "man's highest aspiration for automobiles." The Alfa display became a star attraction at the Italian pavilion and enhanced its reputation for paying the utmost attention to design and form. Carrozzeria Bertone, which was entrusted with the realization of the concept, put Marcello Gandini to work on the task. It had only been one year since he'd taken on design responsibilities at the Turin based carrozzeria, and he had already experienced the

Lamborghini Miura's incredible success at the Salone de Geneva in March of 1966. In August of that same year, taking ideas from the Giulia Sprint GT, he designed a long and low coupé with an extremely innovative shape. A few months later, a full-size model was made. This model was the origin of the two identical prototypes which were unveiled at the Expo in the spring of 1967.

The Alfa Romeo Montreal prototype was an advanced car in many respects. Most of all, its length and width were very unusual for a grand touring car of that time. It was 430 cm long, 173 cm wide and 118 cm tall. The Montreal stood out because of its rigorous equilibrium, which was emphasized by the low lines and the esthetic function of its front grille. The car's frontal design was characterized by horizontal

slats partially covering the headlights, providing a heavily lidded, sexy look. The innovation of incorporating the rear window into the long, truncated tail, the decorative rectangular openings stacked behind the doors, and the accented incline of the front windshield gave the car a striking visual presence.

Although the prototypes were fitted with 1600 cc twin-cam units, the Alfa management envisioned that the Montreal would go into production with a motor which was considerably different from the four cylinder engine for which they were by now famous. By the end of 1966 the technicians at Alfa were already playing with the idea of mounting the spirited V8 motor of the Alfa 33 in this new coupé. Adapting the vehicle to the new mechanical components required extensive reworking of

its dimensions. The presence of the eight cylinder engine and its accompanying transmission forced Bertone to redesign the hood, which became taller and slightly bloated, and to slightly reposition the driver's seat. The height of the car was adjusted and the width was reduced, with resulting changes in the volumetric relationship of the body.

The mechanical aspects, except for the motor, took on the basic design of the other series 105 Alfas including a solid rear axle and four wheel disc brakes. The 90 degree V8 engine was derived straight from the 33 Stradale, though the displacement was increased to 2593 cc (80x64.5 mm). With dual overhead cams per bank, Spica fuel injection, electronic ignition, a dry sump lubrication system, and a compression ratio of 9.3:1, the Montreal produced 200 hp at 6500 rpm. The production version of the Montreal was 422 cm long, 167 cm wide, 120 cm tall, and weighed 1270 kg. It reached a maximum speed of 220 kmph.

The definitive version of the car debuted at the Salon de Geneva in 1970 and would be available for delivery the following year. To the general public, the car seemed very attractive and well built, but the four long years between the debut of the prototype at Expo '67 and its commercial launch on the market was a bad omen for the car. The times were difficult politically as well, and Alfa Romeo had run-ins with the trade unions which were very active in Italy at the time. The Montreal quietly exited the limelight in 1977 after 3,925 of the cars had been built. On these pages, we see a well preserved example of one of these beautiful and exotic GTs.

33 TT 12: WORLD CLASS DESTINY

Alfa Romeo held onto the hope that one day it could achieve its goal of winning the Campionato Mondiale Marche, the World Racing Championship. Their most promising prospect was the Alfa 33/2 and 33/3 which had shown such promise

in the years from 1968 to 1972. In 1970, the technicians at Alfa and Autodelta opted for an aluminum alloy tubular frame in place of the original box structure. The 30 mm diameter tubes would guarantee more rigidity for negotiating the hard turns of the racetrack; while the weight of the frame was kept down to 30 kg, which helped limit that of the entire car to less than 600 kg. In the 1972 season a 2998 cc (86x64.4 mm) V8 engine was installed which increased the power of the car to 440 hp at 9600 rpm. The following year a brand new twelve-cylinder engine was installed to better confront the rivals from Porsche, Matra-Simca, and Ferrari.

From the preceding Alfa 33 the twelve-cylinder version preserved the tubular frame from which it received the initials TT, or "telaio tubolare" in Italian. The wheelbase was 224 cm and the front and rear track were 143 cm and 147 cm respectively. The front suspension was based on that of the earlier model, with triangular arms, coil springs, telescopic shocks, and a roll bar. The rear suspension consisted of upper and lower arms, an anti-sway bar, and two longitudinal reac-

tion struts. The new flat twelve motor was engineered with a very short stroke of only 53.6 mm with a bore of 77 mm to give a displacement of 2995 cc. Its four valves per cylinder, inclined at 35 degrees from each other, were operated by two overhead cams per bank. The block and heads were cast in a light alloy of aluminum and magnesium for a weight of only 178 kg. With Lucas fuel injection and a compression ratio of 11:1 it produced 470 hp at 11,000 rpm. Eventually, in the version prepared for the 1975 season, it achieved 505 hp at 11,500 rpm.

The gearbox, with 5 speeds plus reverse, was mounted in the center between the motor and the differential rather than on a supporting bracket in the rear. This idea, proposed by the engineer Chiti, at Autodelta, helped distribute the weight of the car toward the center. All this attention to detail and performance showed that the technical aspects of the single-seat 33 TT 12 could be compared to the most advanced Formula 1 cars of the era. Its bodywork was the result of the latest experiments in the wind tunnel, while the rear stabilizer and the large air ducts in the front helped control the pressure on the two axles. The form of the car struck a precise balance between the coefficient of drag and the coefficient of lift, which permitted better handling at extremely high speeds.

In 1973, after long sessions of arduous road tests on the racetracks at Balocco, Monza, and Castellet, the 33 TT 12 made a great impression during its short-lived appearance at the 1000 km of Francorchamps. It was 360 cm long, 195 cm

wide, and 96 cm high. The wheels were 9.00/20.0x13 on the front, and 14.0/9.00x13 on the rear. With an empty weight of 670 kg it could reach a maximum speed of 330 kmph.

In the 1973 and 1974 seasons the car competed in many test runs where the performance and reliability of the car were perfected. These qualities became apparent in 1975, allowing Alfa Romeo to win seven of the eight races in which it participated and to clinch the World Championship.

At the 1000 km of Digione, at Monza, Spa, the Coppa Florio, the 1000 km of Nürburgring, Zeltweg, and finally at the Six Hours at Watkins Glen, the formidable 33 TT 12 showed how robust its motor was and how fast it could go. Of these racing cars, only six were produced in total. Like the one seen on these pages from the Alfa Romeo Museo Storico at Arese, the 33 TT 12 remains a precious testimony to the glory of Alfa Romeo.

INDEX